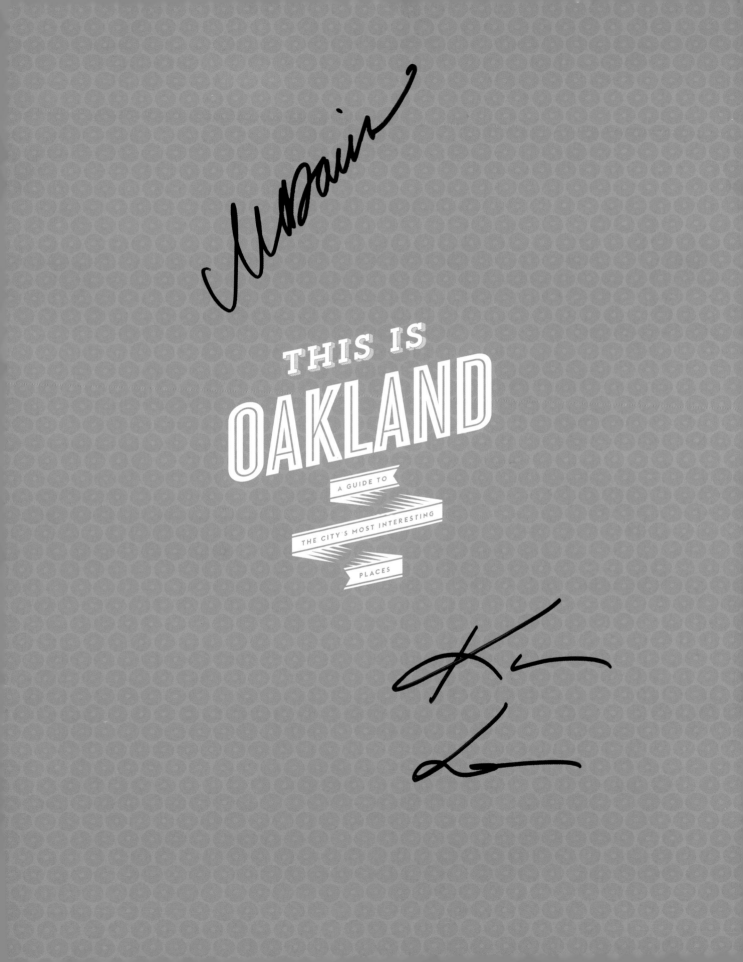

THIS IS
OAKLAND

A GUIDE TO

THE CITY'S MOST INTERESTING

PLACES

This book is for my son, Sammy, who loves going to the Oakland Museum of CA, Fairyland and Fentons Creamery more than anything, and my husband, Sam, who always believes in me.

-Melissa Davis

For my mom, whose love and friendship means everything. And for my dad, whose love of photography and excitement to raise an independent daughter taught me to be fearless in following my dreams. All my love and thanks to you both.

-Kristen Loken

THIS IS
OAKLAND

A GUIDE TO

THE CITY'S MOST INTERESTING

PLACES

MELISSA DAVIS

PHOTOGRAPHY BY KRISTEN LOKEN

ACORN
PRESS

Published by Acorn Press

425 28th Street Unit 201A
Oakland, CA 94609
www.acornpressoakland.com

Visit our website at www.thisisoaklandbook.com

Text copyright © 2014 by Melissa Davis
Photographs copyright © 2014 by Kristen Loken
All rights reserved
Printed and bound in China
First Edition

Book design by Liz Siverts

Library of Congress Cataloging-in-Publication data available.

Every effort has been made to ensure the accuracy of the
information in this book. However, certain details are subject
to change. The publisher cannot accept responsibility for any
consequences arising from use of this book.

ISBN 978-0-9914439-0-1

A couple of years ago, *The New York Times* published a list entitled "The 45 Places to Go in 2012." Oakland, CA ranked #5, between London and Tokyo. It was the highest ranking city in North America. Higher than New York City. Higher than Los Angeles or Oakland's popular older sister, San Francisco. A joke? No way! I assume it was a shock to many—or even most—readers across the country. Perhaps even to those who live in Oakland, but maybe it's because we've become so accustomed to having world-class restaurants, top-notch shopping and architectural gems at our disposal. Sometimes we forget that not every city has so much going for it, with none of the attitude of the usual suspects on those "Where to Go Now" lists.

I moved to Oakland with my husband in 2003, in search of sunshine (believe what you hear about the fog in San Francisco). The sun welcomed me with open arms, as did the melt-in-your mouth donuts at Donut Savant, the perfect-every-time cocktails at Flora, the mouthwatering shrimp tacos at Tamarindo, and the earthy-chic vibe at Atomic Garden (a shop I'd be more than happy to live in, 24/7). Now we're raising our son here, and we love the diversity and creative fun that the city has to offer him. Fairyland, the Oakland Museum of CA and Fentons Creamery... what could be better?

Yes, London and Tokyo have their charms, but the men and women behind the Oakland locales featured here have helped the city earn its ranking on that NYT list. They are the baristas that whip up the perfect latte each morning, or the "treasure hunters" who scour the globe for beautiful treasures so you don't have to. They're creative, inspiring risk-takers, and I'm glad they're my neighbors.

Melissa Davis

JUHU BEACH CLUB

BAKESALE BETTY

51ST ST

MIND'S EYE VINTAGE

PIZZAIOLO

MARISA HASKELL

DOÑA TOMÁS

WALRUS

BOOK/SHOP

ALI GOLDEN

DOUGHNUT DOLLY

TEMESCAL ALLEY BARBER SHOP

CRO CAFÉ

ESQUELETO

CRIMSON HORTICULTURAL RARITIES

STANDARD & STRANGE

49TH ST

BURMA SUPERSTAR

48TH ST

TELEGRAPH AVE

BROADWAY

MASCOT GENERAL STORE

BEAUTY'S BAGEL SHOP

HOMEROOM

ELDER & PINE

HOG'S APOTHECARY

SUBROSA

40TH ST

One of Oakland's hottest destinations, Temescal is known for trend-setting restaurants garnering national attention. And don't miss Temescal Alley: rows of former horse stables now housing some of the city's most innovative shops and services.

DOÑA TOMÁS

"With a last name of Schnetz, people sometimes think I shouldn't be running a Mexican kitchen," says Doña Tomás co-owner and founder Thomas Schnetz. "My grandparents on my mother's side came from Guadalajara and Manzanillo. Rodriguez all the way. Eggs and chorizo."

After graduating from Cal, Tom began working in kitchens and worked his way up. He met partner Dona Savitsky in the restaurant business and they opened their first restaurant, Doña Tomás, together in 1999. Temescal pioneers, the two chose the now-trendy neighborhood because "people barely knew the neighborhood and we were young and foolish enough to assume that people would come from all around. And it had a beautiful patio," explains Tom. The date-friendly Mexican restaurant has a picturesque patio and is known for its carnitas (some customers have ordered nothing but them for 13 years!), the chile rellenos, sopa de lima, and, of course, its margaritas. The two say they have gathered their inspirations from their travels through Mexico, cookbooks and renowned Mexican cook and author Diana Kennedy.

5004 Telegraph Avenue
510 450 0522
donatomas.com

ELDER & PINE

Inspired by his wife's Oakland-based women's vintage shop, Pretty Penny, Nick St. Mary opened his own shop, Elder & Pine. His shop appeals especially to the guy who (let's face it) might sport a beard, enjoy the great outdoors, frequent indie music festivals, and prefer listening to his tunes on vinyl.

Elder & Pine sells vintage clothing and accessories, select new apparel, and hand-picked vintage dry goods, all inspired by camping, free thinkers, motorcycles, and the working-class man. If you're looking for vintage Pendleton flannels, old school tees, and perfectly worn-in work boots, this is your store. A few brands of new apparel and gear round out the assortment, as well as a glass case filled with pocket knives, lighters, belt buckles and the occasional pack of '70s nudie playing cards.

But guys shouldn't shop alone; we've heard that clever women are snatching up the grooming supplies from Prospector Co. for themselves.

423 40th Street
510 420 1980
elderandpine.com

JUHU BEACH CLUB

Juhu Beach is a beach destination in Mumbai known for its high concentration of Bollywood stars' homes and something that beckons to Preeti Mistry on a regular basis: "yummy, snacky, street food," as she calls it. With a wealth of experience under her belt, Preeti, former Executive Chef at Google HQ and the de Young Museum, and Top Chef contestant, opened Juhu Beach Club with partner Ann Nadeau in 2013. Her unique culinary point of view is both Indian and American. The chef explains that she's not setting out to replicate what one would eat in India, rather she is inspired by her experience living in the Bay Area. In fact, when people ask Preeti which Indian region the food is from, she answers, "Oakland."

Preeti found the Bay Area offered little in the way of Indian cuisine other than the traditional Naan N Curry-style joints, and she felt compelled to push the boundaries and create dishes inspired by both her Indian upbringing and her American adolescence, spent eating all types of food. Preeti describes the menu as Indian street food and explains that, "Our food is seasonal and made with care. We make almost everything in house, including all of our masalas that are roasted and ground fresh for all our dishes. The menu is fun for those who want to sample and share many different street food items or come in to have a soul-satisfying dish of their own."

5179 Telegraph Avenue
510 652 7350
juhubeachclub.com

ALI GOLDEN

Ali Golden always knew she'd be her own boss. Her eponymous women's contemporary apparel line is designed and produced in the Bay Area, and she wholesales to boutiques across the country. Customers will often find Ali in the shop, sewing samples or making patterns for her line, which is a chic take on basic pieces. Her clothes can be described as diaphanous in nature and seasonless in feel. They're wearable and cool at the same time. She describes the woman who wears her clothes as, "Someone who wants to look great but also values comfort. The women who buy from my line tell me they appreciate that it's timeless and versatile, and that they can seamlessly transition from day to night in my clothes."

In 2011, a friend introduced Ali to jewelry designer Marisa Haskell, who had recently opened a shop in Temescal Alley. "I immediately fell in love with the neighborhood and was drawn to the community created by the other shop owners," Ali says. "Temescal is brimming with potential and it is very exciting to be a part of and witness the evolving neighborhood."

470 E 49th Street
805 340 7086
aligolden.com

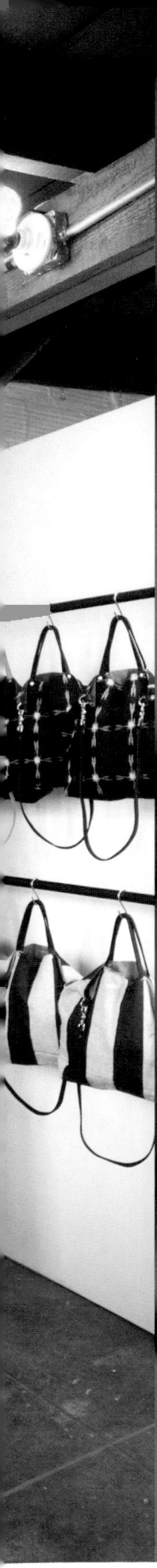

MADE BY HAND
WITH ♥ IN
OAKLAND
THIS BAG WAS CAREFULLY CONSTRUCTED
USING VINTAGE/SCRAP FABRIC
& RECYCLED LEATHER
PLEASE EXCUSE TINY IMPERFECTIONS
WWW.ALIGOLDEN.COM

SINGER

HOMEROOM

In 2011, Allison Arevalo and Erin Wade left their day jobs to follow their calling: opening a mac-n-cheese restaurant. Allison grew up in Brooklyn, cooking alongside her Italian grandmothers. As an adult, she authored a popular food/recipe blog called Local Lemons, which emphasized healthy, natural dishes that took advantage of everything the East Bay has to offer. Erin found her calling as a restaurant critic while studying at Princeton, and found work as a cook before attending law school. The two met by chance in Oakland, and within six months, both left their day jobs to pursue opening Homeroom.

Temescal's Homeroom has a sweet retro school theme, complete with card catalog, paper airplanes and chalkboard, and serves over 10 different varieties of mac-n-cheese at a time—as well as salads, sandwiches, and homemade, old-school style desserts like handmade "oreos" and peanut butter pie. In 2013, they invited the country in on Oakland's little secret with a cookbook that includes recipes for many of the restaurant's favorites, as well as some new treats. Homeroom could cause anyone to look upon their childhood and school days with rose-colored glasses. "How could you dig into a big bowl of cheddary mac and not smile?" laughs Allison.

400 40th Street
510 597 0400
homeroom510.com

MINDS EYE VINTAGE

Business partners Sarah Rainey and Maya Messoriano share a love for traveling and sourcing new finds for their Temescal Alley vintage shop. They refer to themselves as "lifelong treasure hunters" and it seems their loyal clientele appreciates their efforts. Always conscious of how fabrics feel against the skin, Sarah and Maya find that their best selling apparel always seems to be made of cotton, linen or silk. Their customers snap it all up quickly, and they can't seem to keep American-made men's work wear, ankle boots or turquoise jewelry in stock either.

"Being a part of Temescal Alley was an opportunity we couldn't refuse, it's one big family," Sarah says. "We all feed, dress, and inspire each other. The cross pollination is fun and inspiring."

Of Oakland in general, she says, "We love the freedom, variety and lack of pretense that Oakland offers. You can make your own destiny and live your life anyway you choose. No one is looking over your shoulder in Oakland."

486 49th Street
510 529 6519
mindseyevintage.com

MINDS EYE VINTAGE

BEAUTY'S BAGEL SHOP

Amy Remsen and Blake Joffe opened their now-cultishly popular bagel shop after moving to Oakland from Philadelphia and not being able to find authentic, quality bagels. Blake, a former chef, was inspired by the artisanal style in which bagels are made in Montreal, where his father grew up. Amy, who has a range of restaurant experiences under her belt, says, "Blake used to go to Montreal a lot as a kid, and the bagels were a big deal to the family. It was the first and last thing they'd do on a trip." Blake also recalls the bustle of the bagel shops, and seeing the giant wood-burning ovens cooking 24/7.

Although inspired by the Montreal style of bagel making, Amy and Blake call their bagels a sort of hybrid between New York-style and Montreal. "We are really just striving to create our perfect bagel as opposed to being an exact replica of a Montreal bagel shop," says Amy. That being said, they do carry on the tradition of cooking in a large, wood-fired oven. Or perhaps "giant" better describes it at 10,000 pounds. They recall that their bagel oven was delivered in one piece and they actually had to remove part of the building during the four hours it took to move it in. Customers can catch a glimpse of it in action from the counter, as they leave the kitchen doors open for all to see.

3838 Telegraph Avenue
510 788 6098
beautysbagelshop.com

STANDARD & STRANGE

Owners Jeremy Smith and Neil Berrett pulled the name of their menswear shop from Jane Jacobs' *The Death and Life of Great American Cities*. It was appropriate inspiration, given the tome's message about urban development and what makes a city work. After all, the shop is located in charming Temescal Alley, a former Oakland municipal stable brought back to life and an important player in the revitalization of Oakland's vibrant Temescal neighborhood.

Jeremy and Neil's store focuses on American-made men's clothing and accessories, but they've made exceptions for countries with high labor standards such as Canada and Japan. "Our customers range from gardeners to lawyers, but the common thread is that they care about our core values: provenance, quality and timelessness," says Jeremy. Customers can expect to find shirts from Taylor Stitch, belts from Rogue Territory, Dandelion artisanal chocolate bars and notebooks from Rite in the Rain.

484 A 49th Street
510 373 9696
standardandstrange.com

PIZZAIOLO

People in the East Bay often joke that every great new restaurant was started by someone who once worked at Chez Panisse. It's certainly true of Pizzaiolo, where founder Charlie Hallowell was a line cook for almost a decade at Alice Waters' famed Berkeley establishment. When asked why he opened Pizzaiolo, Charlie explains, "I loved cooking at Chez Panisse so much. I loved the philosophy, the beauty, and the sense of family, but it was time for me to make my own family, to create my own aesthetic, and to define the food I wanted to cook..."

When Charlie opened the trend-setting Pizzaiolo in 2005, he lived above the restaurant, which is situated in one of the oldest buildings in Temescal (built in 1897), for six years. He recently bought a house, but he didn't go far; it's only about a mile away. "I love Oakland," says Charlie. "I love the weather, I love the architecture, and I love the breeze off the Bay. Every day I ride my bike to work and I love the walls of smell I get hit with; magnolias in the early spring, jasmine all summer... Oakland is the best smelling city in the world as far as I can tell."

5008 Telegraph Avenue
510 652 4888
pizzaiolooakland.com

TEMESCAL ALLEY BARBER SHOP

Nicholas Vlahos and Bradley Roberts are Temescal Alley pioneers. Back in 2011, they came across the alley when looking for a spot to open an old-school barber shop. Temescal was gaining attention, with restaurants like Bakesale Betty, Doña Tomás and Pizzaiolo attracting local "foodies," but the rents were still affordable. "The neighborhood also lacked the kind of barber shop we envisioned," explains Nick. He and business partner Bradley have been barbers for a combined 15 years and they attract guys (and, sometimes, gals) of all ages and from all walks of life at their shop. "Our customer is the WWII veteran, the baby, the hipster, the First Responder, the soldier, the electrician, the plumber, or the blogger," says Nick. And expect to get an earful at the shop; these guys always have a crazy story to share.

470 B 49th Street
510 761 5074
temescalalleybarbershop.tumblr.com

We believe in the Quality of Vintage. Because the upcycled sol
wood table will be around longer th
the engineered wood table fresh o
the factory floor. We believe in
Creative Re-use. For how else cou
a chair with broken legs become a
swing? We believe in the Perfectl
Imperfect. At Walrus you will not

L'arte

WALRUS

Wendy Renz and Camille Snyder were neighbors in the popular Oakland neighborhood of Rockridge before they became business partners. They discovered each other working on personal furniture projects in their respective backyards, and started to talk. In April 2012, they started selling their upcycled, refurbished and repurposed goods for the home on Etsy and in local flea markets, and opened their tiny shop in Temescal Alley in January 2012. One hundred and sixty-eight square feet might seem absurd and maybe a tad impossible for a store to some, but Wendy and Camille thought it was, well, perfect. They literally fill the space to the rafters with everything from whale-shaped pillows made from vintage fabric to photo display boards made from old picture frames and jute upholstery webbing. Like the goods they sell, they love that their space has a unique history (the retail spaces in the alley were once municipal stables for the horses that pulled the streetcars down Telegraph Avenue). And the sense of community the tiny alley fosters made it quickly feel like home.

470 G 49th Street
510 545 9784
shopwalrus.com

BURMA SUPERSTAR

Burma Superstar owners Desmond Htunlin and wife Jocelyn Lee took a chance when opening their first Burma Superstar in 1992. Bay Area diners may have been unfamiliar with Burmese food, but quickly fell in love with the small nation's cuisine, which takes inspiration from the surrounding countries of Thailand, India and China. Most dishes are composed in a beef, fish or veggie broth, but unlike Thai food, rarely include sugar. Burma Superstar's most popular dishes are the Tea Leaf and Rainbow Salads, kebats (Burmese stir-frys), and addictive coconut rice.

Desmond's family came to the US from Burma in 1979. "I think our dream was very similar to the dream of others who have come to this country from all over the world: to turn hard work into a better life for our family. We arrived as a family of six in San Francisco with less than $200 and limited English, and the journey here was a tough one," he says. Today, Desmond has been able to give back by helping almost 30 refugees find jobs in his trio of restaurants and elsewhere through the International Rescue Committee. "It's been extremely rewarding to see people who arrived in circumstances similar to my family's as they take control of their futures and create more independent lives for themselves and their families."

4721 Telegraph Avenue
510 652 2900
burmasuperstaroakland.com

MASCOT GENERAL STORE

"I have been obsessed with thrift shops, estate sales, and flea markets since I was a kid," confesses owner Abigail McCannon. "I remember begging my mom to take me to the local Goodwill when I was a teenager. I just love the rush of the score!" Abi studied fashion design, but followed her heart when she started her vintage business. She tested the waters with an online shop, and when her customers wanted more, she opened the Mascot General Store in 2012.

Abi's shop reflects her well-trained eye and instinct. She blends an interesting mix of vintage home décor which includes old globes, wool blankets, mid-century lamps, vintage apothecary bottles, paperbacks from the '70s, and vinyl records, and yet the collection feels remarkably cohesive and beautifully curated. (Did we mention she wraps purchases in vintage sewing patterns?)

4124 Broadway
510 788 4477
mascotgeneralstore.com

CRO CAFÉ

Family inspires CRO Café owner Luigi Oldani. The coffee shop is named after his 14-year-old daughter Camille Rosemary Oldani and it was the loss of his father that drove him to quit his engineering job and start his own business. Part artist, part engineer, Luigi had a vision for CRO Café that was so much more than just a coffee shop. He was just as inspired by the machinery as he was the coffee itself. "I fell hopelessly in love with coffee and everything that went with it... the wonderful gear (you can't make espresso without a machine!), the fanaticism and incredible attention to detail needed to prepare such a volatile beverage, and of course, the 'foodie' side of it. After all, the best machines don't guarantee good coffee, they just enable it. Your starting point has to be a high-quality, organic product and you need to respect it as such," explains Luigi.

He sold coffee with a mobile coffee cart (that he built himself) before opening in 2012 in Temescal Alley. While he loves his current location, Luigi has plans for expansion in the future, which may include multiple locations, a workshop and art gallery, and a mobile truck that promises to knock Oakland's socks off.

470 49th Street
510 658 6839
thecrocafe.com

ESQUELETO

Jewelry designer Lauren Wolf studied silversmithing in Mexico, and finished her studies at Fashion Institute of Technology in New York City, where she launched her line. Lauren moved to Oakland in 2010 with her then boyfriend (an Oakland native) and when she was ready to open a shop, spent about a year and a half waiting to find the perfect spot. "I've been designing the Lauren Wolf Jewelry Collection for the past 10 years and I was ready to add a different element to the business by opening a retail location," explains the designer. "It just made sense to sell directly to our customer base and have the opportunity to showcase the work of so many talented, local artists."

The beautiful, light-filled corner Temescal Alley space sells Lauren's own textural, organic line as well as a large assortment of other jewelry and accessory designers' work and also uses the space to showcase (often local) art.

482 A 49th Street
510 629 6216
shopesqueleto.com

BAKESALE BETTY

If you see a line of hungry people snaking around Telegraph Avenue at lunchtime, you can bet they are waiting to snatch up a fried chicken sandwich and strawberry shortcake from Oakland institution Bakesale Betty. Owner Alison Barakat opened the shop in 2005, and within a year word had spread like wildfire. Today, Bakesale Betty's Buttermilk Fried Chicken Sandwich may be the most popular sandwich the city has ever seen. She tells us she serves about 500-600 of them a day, and the city never seems to tire of the delectable lunch. It seems simple enough—combine an Acme roll, free range fried chicken, and a spicy secret slaw—but Alison's creation has inspired national attention and copycats spanning the country.

The Chez Panisse alum started Bakesale Betty at the local farmer's market, simply selling sweet baked goods, which are still standouts at the shop. The charming staff is always happily buzzing with activity behind the counter and makes the wait worthwhile; they've been known to hand out cookies to patrons as they wait or slip an extra cookie or two into their bags. But don't come to Bakesale Betty expecting a fine dining experience. Customers either take their sandwiches to go in a brown bag or eat elbow-to-elbow at a stool and retro ironing board (a.k.a. makeshift table) on the sidewalk, which is all part of the fun.

5098 Telegraph Avenue
510 985 1213
bakesalebetty.com

CRIMSON HORTICULTURAL RARITIES

Allison Futeral and Lonna Lopez use the word "community" a lot. It's why they opened their shop and it's what they believe sustains it. Crimson is not only a boutique selling a variety of exquisite horticultural finds, but also a storefront for the business partners' floral and garden design business. They regularly welcome a variety of shoppers, from those who want to buy a unique bouquet of fresh flowers to couples interested in wedding arrangements, to locals looking for a place to learn and find inspiration. Both Allison and Lonna love being a part of the Temescal community and connecting with neighbors, teaching them about plants and flowers.

Their shop is a feast for the senses. The walls and shelves are filled with an abundance of succulents and tillandsia, natural curiosities including taxidermy birds and preserved pheasant wings, vintage gardening books, Santa Maria Novella fragrances for the home and body, and hand-made preserves made by Lonna.

470 49th Street
510 992 3359
crimsonhort.com

BOOK/SHOP

After dabbling in online retail, blogging, and pop-up shops, Erik Heywood opened Book/Shop in Temescal Alley. Erik explains, "The rawness of the space lends itself to feeling 'unpolished' which opens up a feeling of possibility and frees me up to keep messing with the space, which I do constantly!"

Book/Shop is not a traditional bookseller, but as Erik explains, "A shop about books. We try to help people slow down and think about them. It's about making books a part of your life. The books that we sell are primarily vintage books in exceptional condition, sourced from rare book dealers and collectors, and we only have about 80 or so books in the shop at a time. We work hard to curate a collection of 'gems,' all the time. We change the 'curation' of books every two weeks, meaning that every time someone comes into the shop, it's essentially a new shop, with extraordinary books every time." Books range from $10 to $500, but Book/Shop is never about tomes too precious to touch.

The former Brooklynite says of his new Oakland shop, "We hope we're seen as a good addition to the remarkable things happening in Oakland right now. It feels a little like Brooklyn in the late '90s/early 2000s in that everyone else seemed to get that Brooklyn was the new place to be, way before people in Manhattan understood it. I have people in San Francisco tell me flatly that they'll never come to Oakland, but I have people constantly coming in from New York, London, Tokyo, etc, who've rented a car in San Francisco specifically to come to Book/Shop."

482 D 49th Street
510 907 9649
book---shop.com

46

HOG'S APOTHECARY

Owners Bradford Earle and John Streit once lived at opposing ends of the 40th Street corridor in Temescal, and walked the stretch to each other's homes frequently. They noticed that there was a large community that was woefully underserved when it came to local food and beer options. They found a space between them that had the right bones, and the two combined their talents and backgrounds to create Hog's Apothecary in 2013. Their concept? Bradford tells us, "We like to call Hog's Apothecary an American Beer Hall. We wanted to evoke the communal nature of the European beer halls while putting our own twist on it. Our ethos is summed up by our motto 'Locavore meets Loca-pour.'" Hog's carries thirty-two beers, one cider, five wines, and one root beer on draft and about fifteen to twenty beers by the bottle. They focus on locally crafted beers, coming from breweries no further then San Diego to the south and Seattle to the north.

The menu carries the same local philosophy; all of their food is sourced from local farms and they are committed to whole animal butchery, with no parts of the animal going to waste. The menu varies day to day, but expect house-made sausages and other hearty main dishes.

375 40th Street
510 338 3847
hogsapothecary.com

DOUGHNUT DOLLY

Many a chef claim to have grown up in the kitchen, but few can say they grew up in the kitchen of Chez Panisse, as Doughnut Dolly owner Hannah Hoffman did. Hannah's mother, Lisa Goines, was a pastry chef at Alice Waters' world-renowned Berkeley restaurant from 1971 to 1987. A photo of Lisa in the Chez Panisse kitchen with baby Hannah at her side now hangs on the wall of Hannah's enticing doughnut shop.

Starting at the age of 14, Hannah learned how to do it all, from pastry and line cooking to recipe testing and wine pairing. Customers can taste her expertise in the hand rolled, yeast-raised doughnuts she makes daily, each filled to order with one (or a combo) of the four filling choices for the day. The Naughty Cream—a crème-fraîche vanilla bean pastry cream—is always on the menu, and customers will always find a chocolate option (like Mexican chocolate) and jam option.

482 B 49th Street
510 338 6738
doughnutdolly.com

ALLEY 49 DOUGHNUT DOLLY

FAT TUESDAY!
"Naughty Cream"
Wild Plum Jam
Bourbon Cream

SUBROSA

Catherine Macken has lived in North Oakland since 2000, and immediately fell in love with the tiny (110 sq feet!) space that now houses her charming coffee shop. "I wasn't sure that the space could accommodate a coffee shop, so I followed my dad's advice and mocked up the space with cardboard counters before moving forward with the design. It was awesome; we made every inch count."

Subrosa sells Fourbarrel coffee, brewed by hand, and is staffed with musicians, artists and writers who all share a love of coffee. The coffee outpost may be tiny, but it's bright and cheerful, with reclaimed fir flooring set off by creamy concrete and subway tiles. When asked what she loves most about Oakland, the former designer says, "It's cool. It's mysterious. What's not to love?"

419 40th Street
510 740 8020
subrosacoffee.com

MARISA HASKELL

Jewelry designer and shop owner Marisa Haskell can't quite pinpoint exactly who her customer is. "It's a broad range of people that come into the shop," she explains. "But I do think that all of my customers appreciate buying jewelry that was made in the same space where they are buying it."

Marisa's jewelry is, by her description, feminine but with a bit of a rough edge. She works in brass and some rose bronze and is drawn to both raw, natural stones and bold shapes. Delicate necklaces are meant to be layered and bolder pieces stand on their own. Marisa never studied jewelry design, but growing up in Santa Barbara with antique dealer parents, paired with a background in painting, fine-tuned her aesthetic and sense of design. She opened her Temescal Alley shop in 2011 and was drawn to the semi-private nature of being tucked away down the pedestrian-only alley. "It has that private feeling that allowed me to make my shop really personal and leave it a little rough around the edges," Marisa says.

470D 49th Street
510 325 0019
marisahaskell.com

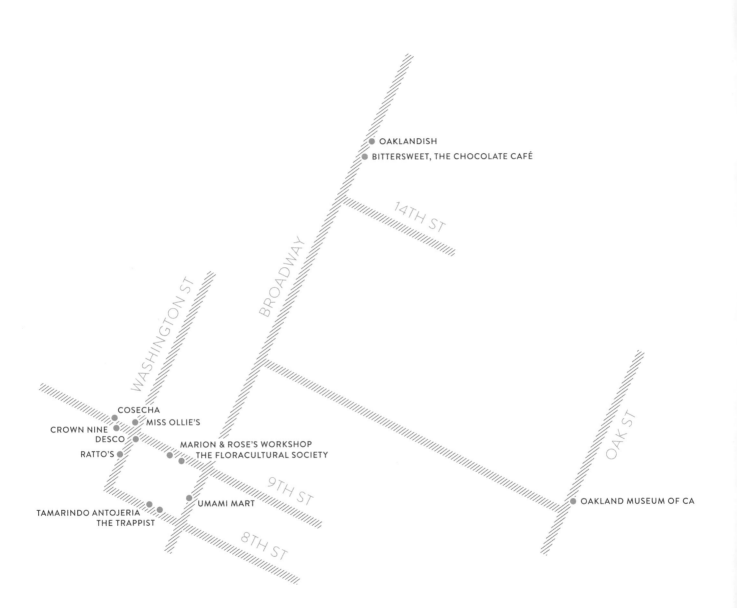

OAKLANDISH

BITTERSWEET, THE CHOCOLATE CAFÉ

14TH ST

BROADWAY

WASHINGTON ST

OAK ST

COSECHA

CROWN NINE

MISS OLLIE'S

DESCO

RATTO'S

MARION & ROSE'S WORKSHOP
THE FLORACULTURAL SOCIETY

9TH ST

UMAMI MART

TAMARINDO ANTOJERIA
THE TRAPPIST

8TH ST

OAKLAND MUSEUM OF CA

A neighborhood rich with history, what is now called Old Oakland was the final west coast stop of the Central Pacific Railroad in the 1800s. As a result, this was the city's first business center. The area, within Oakland's downtown, is regaining its former glory with great eateries and shops moving into revitalized historic buildings.

OAKLANDISH

Oaklandish started in 2000 as a public art project by Jeff Hull and Angela Tsay celebrating "local love and original Oakland charm." Eleven years later, Angela opened their retail store in the heart of downtown Oakland, and inadvertently triggered a revitalization of the neighborhood. The store features Oaklandish's clever civic pride apparel, plus wares from over one hundred local makers. Angela explains, "We moved to the heart of downtown Oakland because we wanted to challenge how people perceive the neighborhood. We wanted to update the so-often negative perception of downtown Oakland with something that was closer to the reality of the city. This corridor was once the bustling commercial center of the East Bay. It's where your grandma took you for holiday shopping and then ice cream for special occasions. We wanted to harken back to that."

Bestsellers include their t-shirts and hoodies with Oakland-referenced graphics, but shoppers can also expect to find unique wares from local artists and makers ranging from soaps to jewelry to chocolate. Says Angela, "Our t-shirts might be the most visible part of Oaklandish, but our community work is the reason we do what we do. It's our way of giving back to the city that gives so much to the world, and it informs every decision we make."

Oaklandish gives a portion of its proceeds to grassroots organizations through grants, donations, pro bono design work, and marketing support, with 10% of proceeds from collaborative designs earmarked for local nonprofits.

1444 Broadway
510 251 9500
oaklandish.com

DESCO

Donato Scotti was looking to open his second Italian restaurant somewhere in the East Bay, but when he came across the spectacular corner space in Old Oakland, he looked no further. "I love the feel of the building and the warmth of the restaurant with the original brick work," he says about the restaurant, which is housed in one of the oldest buildings in the city (built in 1876). "Old Oakland is an up-and-coming culinary destination with history and charm."

Breathtakingly huge windows frame the space and portions of century-old tile flooring still exist in the space today. Slide onto a stool at the copper-topped bar, or join a friend at a table and indulge in homemade pastas and unique regional dishes from Italy. "Our most popular dish is Casonei, a ravioli with brown butter sauce and sage from my hometown of Bergamo," says Donato, but of course their Neapolitan-style pizzas fired in a wood-burning oven also lure hungry Oaklanders.

499 9th Street
510 663 9000
descooakland.com

RATTO'S
SANDWICHES

o The Jenny (v)
o Avocado & Pepper Jack (v)
o Hummus (v)
o Italiano Combo
o Turkey & Avocado

60

RATTO'S

Giovanni Battista Ratto opened G.B. Ratto & Co. International Grocers in 1897, in Oakland, not far from their current location on Washington Street. In 1936, G.B.'s son bought the building in which Ratto's still stands, had an Italian craftsman pour a lustrous green terrazzo floor, and moved the popular Oakland grocer into the storefront space. The business is currently family-owned and run by G.B.'s great grand-daughter, Elena Durante.

Ratto's remains an Oakland destination to this day, focusing on globally imported gourmet foods from Europe, the Middle East and Africa. Back in the 1960s, 70s and 80s, Ratto's was known for its vast selection of bulk herbs, spices, grains, rice, beans, legumes, and specialty flours, but cheeses and charcuterie have always stolen the show. "Today, though we do still sell imported gourmet groceries, imported and domestic cheeses and charcuterie, we are mainly a deli that cater to the local lunch crowd. We sell great deli sandwiches, salads and soups," Elena explains.

She tells us, "Of the many pleasurable encounters I have with my customers, the ones that often stand out the most are when a customer tells me stories about coming to the store as a child with their parents or grandparents. On the flip side, it also makes me just as happy when someone comes in the store for the first time and tells me how nice the shop is, and that they loved their lunch and will be back..."

821 Washington Street
510 832 6503
rattos.com

OAKLAND MUSEUM OF CA

Award-winning architect Kevin Roche and landscape architect Dan Riley designed the mid-century modern Oakland Museum of California to have three levels of galleries focusing on three independent disciplines—art, history, and natural sciences—with lush gardens at each level. The museum opened in 1969, and received a complete overhaul of its galleries between 2010 and 2013, when collections were brought to life by innovative, interactive features that encourage participation from museum guests. What has not changed is the museum's goal: to celebrate all facets of California, from its rich history to its role in the world today.

Truly interactive and fun for visitors of all ages, the museum also hosts family-friendly "Friday Nights @ OMCA" each week, when the museum stays open until 9 PM, with half price admission (and kids under 18 are free), and a range of fun activities including live music, DJs, hands-on art workshops, beer, wine and Off the Grid food trucks, as well as story time for the kids and guest speakers for the adults.

1000 Oak Street
510 318 8400
museumca.org

COSECHA

Dominica Rice-Cisneros was inspired by the space Cosecha occupies in Oakland's historic Swan's Market because it reminded her of the indoor markets that are so common in Mexico. "Cosecha means harvest," she explains. "We are a Mexican restaurant with a California influence. We use local ingredients as much as we can and develop relationships with farmers and growers. The food style, however, is very inspired by Southern Mexico—especially the Distrito Federal—or Mexico City. We don't smother our food with sour cream or cheese. We try to let the real flavors of the chile, maiz, and frijoles come through."

Dominica inherited her love of Mexican cooking from her grandmother, who came to the States from Chihuahua during the Mexican Revolution. Today, locals and visitors who are more than willing to wait in line for Cosecha's wild shrimp tacos, pork belly tacos, and pretty much anything made with their freshly made tortillas, know who to thank.

907 Washington Street
510 452 5900
cosechacafe.com

THE FLORACULTURAL SOCIETY

Owner Anna Campbell has a unique approach to her flower shop. As she tells us, "FloraCultural Society is about recon-necting the consumer to where flowers come from, much like the farm-to-table movement in food. We grow rare and heirloom cut flowers for the shop... In an urban setting, I feel like you're always trying to reconnect to the green spaces while enjoying the concrete jungle, so vases of sweet peas do make a difference. We're always trying to 'rewild' our lives."

With a background at *Martha Stewart Weddings*, Stanlee R. Gatti Designs, and Anthropologie, she has a well-trained eye and has created a charming shop in Old Oakland's historic Gladstone Building. "This was one of the first blocks I fell in love with when we moved to Oakland. It feels like you've en-tered another part of the world. Our business model and name is based on the flowers, crafts and traditions of yesteryear. We also have a farm just two blocks east in the Acorn District which still has traces from when it was the flower district for Oakland. We'd like to bring flowers back to what was once a prolific trade in the area," explains Anna.

461A 9th Street
415 608 2040
floraculturalsociety.com

THE
FloraCultural
SOCIETY

Rewild Your Life...

HEIRLOOM AND RARE
FLOWER CUTTINGS

BOTANICAL GOODS

CLASSES AND EVENTS

Flower Menu:

1. jaunty daffodil

2. sweet pea

3. clementines

4. foxtail

5. poppies

6. mixed tropicals

THE TRAPPIST

A culmination of their passion for beer and years of beer-oriented travels, Aaron Porter and Chuck Stilphen opened The Trappist in an 1870s Victorian in 2007. Inspired by the greatest European pubs, the bar's name refers to tradition of Belgian and Dutch Trappist monks brewing beer to fund monasteries. Aaron tells us, "The beer selection is all about what's best, what we like, and the breweries we respect. We only offer what we feel is best and what we are excited about." As their customers come from all around the globe, they are a destination, and yet still very much a loved, local bar. They always take great care and pride in the handling and treatment of the beer and food that they serve.

The bar has expanded since its opening and now includes an outdoor patio and back bar, which made their food program possible. The menu has also evolved from simple meat and cheese plates to fare best described as California Bistro Pub, which features the best local ingredients.

460 8th Street
510 238 8900
thetrappist.com

UMAMI MART

It all began with a blog. Umami Mart owners Kayoko Akabori and Yoko Kumano first started a food blog by the same name while they were living across the globe from each other, in Brooklyn and Tokyo, respectively. The blog quickly became a popular destination for writers from around the world to discuss food and drink, and in 2010, they decided to open an online store. Two years later, after moving back to their native SF Bay Area, they opened the Umami Mart brick and mortar shop in a charming 1890s building in Oakland's Old Oakland. Their chic, modern Japanese kitchen and barware shop is a favorite of local editors and bloggers, and shoppers snatch up their spherical ice cube trays, gold barware, and elegant crystal glasses. Umami Mart's fun "conbini" (convenience store) in the back of the shop stocks Japanese snacks, drinks and magazines.

Yoko says, "Our community is very important to us. We hold events at least once a month in our space. Those events give us an opportunity to welcome our regulars and talk to the community. We also sell bento and onigiri (rice balls) every weekday that we're open."

815 Broadway
510 250 9559
umamimart.com

MISS OLLIE'S

In 2013, Afro-Caribbean restaurant Miss Ollie's opened in Oakland's historic Swan's Market, which dates back to the early twentieth century. Co-owner and chef, Sarah Kirnon, tells us, "Growing up in the Caribbean, the market was and is a big part of island life so when I saw the space at Swan's, it felt very fitting." She was raised in Barbados by her grandmother, "Miss Ollie," who was the inspiration behind much of the menu and the name of the restaurant.

"We serve foods related to the African Diaspora, and our menu is heavily influenced by the Caribbean with nods to Africa and the American South," says Sarah. "We have very strong support from the Afro-Caribbeans that reside here, which is beautiful. When I look at our customers as a whole, though, it seems to just be a great, eclectic group of people."

The menu typically offers salt fish & ackee, plantains and garlic oil, and sugarcane-grilled jerk hen, but it's Sarah's crispy and tender fried chicken that keeps Oakland buzzing.

901 Washington Street
510 285 6188
missolliesoakland.com

MARION & ROSE'S WORKSHOP

Marion & Rose's Workshop is named after owner Kerri Johnson's grandmother. When Johnson opened her shop in 2011, she strove to create an environment like that of her grandmother's era. Explains Kerri, "People who visit my shop appreciate craftsmanship, and are seeking out unique items that are fashioned by the hands of a skilled maker. They enjoy buying products with a story, and they can often find me sharing stories about the makers I work with and their process. It's also somewhat of a workshop where people can meet local makers and artists, see demonstrations, enjoy trunk shows, and even sample some of the food items we sell."

Marion & Rose's Workshop sells happy American-made goods for the home, person and pet. Kerri seeks out heirloom quality goods from artisans and companies who produce products on a small scale, and have ethical manufacturing processes... and she earns bonus points for keeping prices affordable. Shoppers can expect to find letterpress cards and art prints, wrapping papers, blankets, handmade ceramic pottery and charming kitchen linens.

461 9th Street
510 214 6794
marionandrose.com

BITTERSWEET, THE CHOCOLATE CAFÉ

Most of us love chocolate, but Bittersweet Café owners Penelope Finnie and Diana Meckfessel are crazy about chocolate. They opened the first of their three East Bay cafes in 2005, with the downtown Oakland location opening in 2012. The two were inspired to create a chocolate-oriented café from their travels, and as Penelope tells us, "We started as a 'wine store' for chocolate, a place that focused on the agricultural roots of chocolate. We were eager to make fine chocolates less intimidating, and not just a luxury item." In addition to selling high-end chocolate bars from around the globe, they also sold chocolate drinks. Of course, you can't have a café focused on chocolate without baked goods, and the business has grown and morphed over the years.

What has not changed is their dedication to bringing their customers a high-quality, artisanal chocolate and coffee experience. Bittersweet roasts their own coffee on the premises, makes small batch bean-to-bar chocolate, grinds their own hot chocolate mixes and of course bakes their scrumptious chocolate-oriented bakery goods in-house. We love that the café also caters to the downtown lunch crowd, with tasty homemade fried chicken sandwiches, soup, and fresh salads.

1438 Broadway
510 238 8700
bittersweetcafe.com

CROWN NINE

Crown Nine, Kate Ellen's flagship jewelry boutique, stocks her eponymous jewelry line, Kate Ellen Metals, alongside a rotating roster of coveted independent jewelry makers. As Kate explains, "We also carry handmade glass works, fragrance, leather, and ceramics. We believe in real, beautiful things made by real people."

Kate Ellen Metals reflects her obsession with materials and metals. Known for a hand-wrought look with lots of texture and detailing, Kate's pieces tend to strike a delicate balance between organic and industrial; bold yet natural. Engagement and wedding rings are her number one seller, and as Kate tells us, "It is an honor to be involved in such an intimate thing, and I really relish the process. I love getting to celebrate love each and every day in my work."

Located within the historic Ratto's building, the shop is in the former carriage house built in the 1870's. Kate's workshop is in the upstairs loft, and the retail space is on the ground level. "Being a part of Old Oakland, the original downtown of the city, and connected to that time in history is a blast," says Kate.

515 9th Street
510 507 0789
crown-nine.com

TAMARINDO ANTOJERIA

In 2005, Tamarindo Antojeria opened its doors in Old Oakland, in one of the very first downtown buildings in the city, dating back to the 1800s. Mother and son duo, Gloria and Alfonso Dominguez, are passionate about Oakland and providing the city with authentic, mouth-watering Mexican food in a stylish environment. Gloria is the restaurant's chef, and Alfonso, an architect, designed the space. "Memory of food is important here at Tamarindo," Gloria says. "We wanted Mexican people that live here in the US to have a place to come and eat exactly what they would in Mexico, or what their grandmother would have cooked for them."

Gloria and her husband moved to Oakland from their native Mexico when they were teenagers; her son Alfonso is American born. He and Gloria opened the restaurant soon after Alfonso moved back to Oakland following his graduation from college. The neighborhood of Old Oakland was a natural fit for the two, with its impressive original architecture and historic charm. Offering delicious street food and small plates from various regions of Mexico, Tamarindo has become a staple in the neighborhood scene.

468 8th Street
510 444 1944
tamarindoantojeria.com

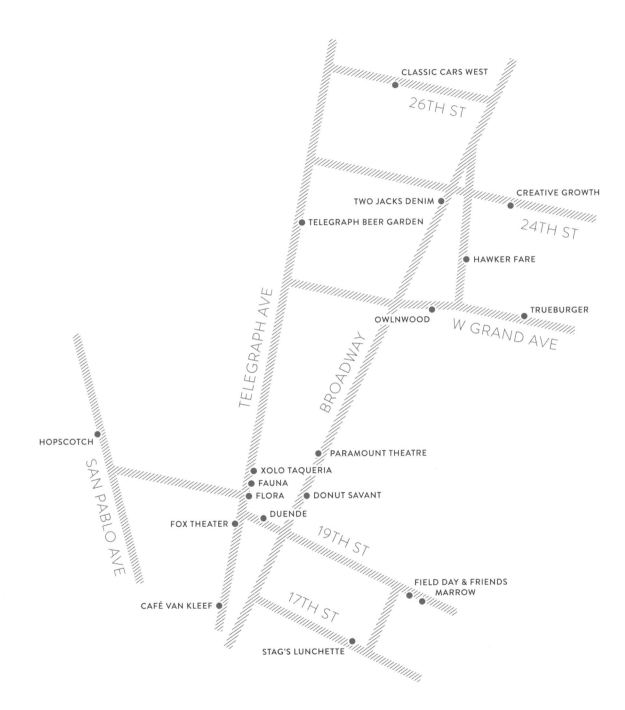

CLASSIC CARS WEST

26TH ST

CREATIVE GROWTH

TWO JACKS DENIM

24TH ST

TELEGRAPH BEER GARDEN

HAWKER FARE

TELEGRAPH AVE

TRUEBURGER

OWLNWOOD

W GRAND AVE

BROADWAY

HOPSCOTCH

PARAMOUNT THEATRE

SAN PABLO AVE

XOLO TAQUERIA

FAUNA

FLORA

DONUT SAVANT

DUENDE

FOX THEATER

19TH ST

FIELD DAY & FRIENDS

MARROW

CAFÉ VAN KLEEF

17TH ST

STAG'S LUNCHETTE

Uptown is Oakland's entertainment district, boasting live music venues, cool bars, and inventive restaurants, all of which are inspiring the rest of the city and country. The neighborhood's spectacular renovated movie palaces—the Fox and the Paramount—are brilliant reminders of the city's past.

FLORA
AND FAUNA

Thomas Schnetz and Dona Savitsky opened Flora in Oakland's Uptown neighborhood years before it was named one of country's hippest 'hoods by *Forbes* magazine. It was in 2007 that they moved into the classic Art Deco building that originally housed the Oakland Floral Depot. The cobalt-glazed terra cotta tiles and ornate silver accents still stand from the '30s, as does the old neon "flora" sign. The charm carries through inside the restaurant, which feels like a classic American eatery from a simpler time. Tufted leather banquets, crisp white tablecloths and a large bar set the backdrop for American fare with a modern twist, and service that's always warm and charming. The restaurant quickly became known for its handcrafted cocktails and in 2012, Tom and Dona opened the bar Fauna next door. Fauna is a little darker, a little sexier, and definitely more playful. It's the perfect spot to hang out and wait for a table at Flora, or to just meet a date for well-made cocktails.

1900 Telegraph Avenue
510 286 0100
floraoakland.com and faunaoakland.com

FIELD DAY AND FRIENDS

In 2005, owner Trinity Cross created her women's apparel line, Field Day. Dedicated to sustainability, she uses organic cotton, bamboo, and reclaimed textiles, including high thread count vintage sheets, which are washed and sun dried. Every piece on the line is dyed, sewn and printed one at a time, locally, in Oakland. Trinity lives by her credo; she lives on a small urban farm in West Oakland, where she grows vegetables and raises chickens, bees, and rabbits and her shop was thoughtfully built out in 2013 using reclaimed materials. Trinity explains, "Using reclaimed and recycled materials was a big part of what made the space feel loved and cherished. I love giving new life to all things discarded."

The "friends" in the store name refers to the other lines she carries. Shoppers can expect to find a carefully chosen array of charming handmade products, from locally made jewelry, beeswax candles, local honey, handmade brooms, tinctures, and bath and body products. And its no surprise that ninety percent of the brands Field Day and Friends carries are made right here in the Bay Area.

329 19th Street
510 338 6624
fielddayandfriends.com

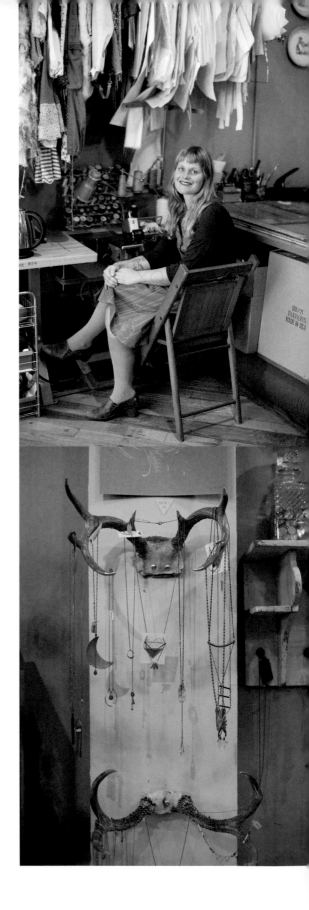

CAULDRON POLISH
cold care elixir

A potent blend
of health-full herbs
to charm away the
most callous of colds.

WORTS & CUNNING
APOTHECARY

field day
&
friends
handcrafted boutique

HAWKER FARE

Chef/owner James Syhabout, one of Oakland's top chefs, is the owner of Michelin-rated Commis as well as newcomer Box and Bells, but the food he cooks at Hawker Fare is especially close to his heart. Inspired by food his mother made throughout his childhood, the menu is based on Southeast Asian street food. (A "hawker" is a street food vendor.) He loves a rice-bowl, but James applies innovative twists to these seemingly simple dishes, and in true Oakland fashion, creates them from the best local, sustainable, and organic ingredients.

The space features a graffiti-art mural and has a cool, urban vibe, and the food is just as vibrant. The Papaya Som Tum is a flavorful starter and customers are crazy about the 24hr Pork Belly and Kao Mun Gai rice bowls. Add a Mexican Coke or quenching Doug Re-Fresh cocktail (gin, cucumber simple syrup and a splash of lemon juice) and you're set.

2300 Webster Street
510 832 8896
hawkerfare.com

CREATIVE GROWTH

In 1974, Florence and Elias Katz invited newly de-institution-
alized men and women with disabilities to express themselves
through art. The couple, an artist and a psychologist respectively, invited these burgeoning artists into their garage, where
they set up tables with art supplies and urged these men and
women to put paintbrush to paper. Those humble beginnings
have grown into a 10,000 square foot space in Oakland's
Uptown neighborhood which houses a light-filled professional
art studio for over 140 artists, an art gallery showing selected
work, and a small shop selling their wares. Creative Growth
sees its role as fostering the personal and artistic development
of its artists, some of which have gone on to have work featured in notable galleries and museums, including the perma-
nent collections of New York City's MOMA.

Creative Growth artists work in a variety of media, including
pencil, pastels, paint, mosaics, ceramics, textiles, fiber arts,
wood, video, and printmaking. Each artist develops a working
portfolio. The program also brings the artists out of the studio
for inspiring trips to museums, galleries, and other artists'
studios. The work that Creative Growth has done to challenge
stereotypes about disabilities has inspired over 25 similar pro-
grams around the world.

355 24th Street
510 836 2340
creativegrowth.org

$2.50

Rosemary
Shortbread

VEGGIE "CHICKEN" SUB $11
VEGGIE 'CHICKEN' MEAT
HEIRLOOM ROMA
TOMATO SAUCE, SALSA VERDE
SLICED MOZZ AND PROVOLONE

SMOKED

HOUSE SM
SUN-DRIED

PASTRAMI REUBEN $10
DOUBLE MEAT $15
SMOKED ORGANIC BRISKET
GRUYERE CHEESE
PIQUANT DRESSING SPICY
HOUSE KRAUT

VEAL AND BEEF $12
MEATBALL
5 DOT BEEF AND VEAL
RICOTTA MEATBALLS
HEIRLOOM ROMA
TOMATO SAUCE
SLICED MOZZ AND PROVOLONE
BASIL SALSA VERDE

MEXICAN CHICKEN $11
CLUB
ACHIOTE RUBBED ROSIES
CHICKEN THIGH
THIN SLICED HOUSE BACON
SHAVED MEXICAN CHEESE
AVOCADO CILANTRO SALAD
PICKLED PASSILLAS
FRESNO MARJORAM AIOLI

GRILLED L
GRILLED CORN AN
SALAD WITH
GARLIC AIOLI
PARSLEY CRE

STAG'S LUNCHETTE

It's hard to believe that owner Alexeis Filipello was a teenage vegetarian. "I wasn't very good at it," she laughs. Stag's Lunchette, a breakfast and lunch joint on a tree-lined street in Oakland's Uptown district, is a haven for meat-lovers. The menu changes weekly (check their Facebook page each Tuesday) but what remains the same is Lexi's dedication to cruelty-free, hormone-free, and antibiotic-free meats. She smokes her own pastrami, cures her own bacon, and even roasts suckling pigs on the rotisserie. Prices are more than fair for the quality of the food: hearty lunch entrees typically don't top $12 and portions are generous.

The tiny eatery filled with antlers, taxidermy, and bell jars has a hip, rustic lodge feel, but attracts all types for breakfast and lunch. Lines snake out the door and customers clamor for a bar stool or a seat at one of the few tables, but it's all worth it.

362 17th Street
510 835 7824
stagslunchette.com

HOPSCOTCH

Mix Jenny Schwarz's beautifully crafted cocktails and front-of-house expertise with chef Kyle Itani's years of restaurant experience ranging from San Francisco's Yoshi's to The Meatball Shop in New York, and you have a winning combination. The two friends opened Hopscotch on an quiet block in Oakland's quickly growing Uptown neighborhood in 2012 and the tiny restaurant has been packing in happy patrons ever since.

Kyle's American menu is peppered with interesting Japanese influences, yet manages to remain unassuming and approachable. His buttermilk fried chicken with seasonal sides has attracted such a following that what was supposed to be a brief appearance on the menu became a Hopscotch staple. The interior also has a few twists; the retro 1950s diner-influenced space, with red leather diner chairs and a checkerboard floor, is offset by classic touches like wainscoting and a gorgeous marble bar. Hopscotch feels like a neighborhood spot that's been there forever, and we hope it will be.

1915 San Pablo Avenue
510 788 6217
hopscotchoakland.com

PARAMOUNT THEATRE

Oakland's art deco gem, the Paramount Theatre, was designed by the architectural firm of J.R. Miller and T.L. Pflueger, although Timothy Pflueger was most responsible for its noteworthy design. The prolific architect was joined by several talented artists and designers who brought the theater to life just two short years after the start of the Great Depression. Oaklanders flocked to see movies in the exceptional movie palace for its first two decades in business, but when the city-dwellers started to move out to the suburbs in the 50s, the crowds waned, and the theater faced years of neglect.

In 1972, the Paramount was purchased by the Board of Directors of the Oakland Symphony Orchestra Association, and in 1973, a painstaking renovation was completed. The city took over in 1975, and the theatre is now home to the Oakland East Bay Symphony, Oakland Ballet Company and hosts a variety of shows, concerts, theater productions and classic movies. In addition to its lively events calendar, the tours of this Oakland institution—offered twice a month—are not to be missed.

2025 Broadway
510 465 6400
paramounttheatre.com

Served w/ Grilled ... $1
verde + a 65° egg

THE DEAL $9.17

2.5" Grass-Fed Patty Served
w/ American Cheese, Romaine, Shaved
Onion + Oven Dried Tomatoes on
A toasted A.B.C. Potato Bun.
Comes w/ Fries And a Drink of
your choice.....

DESSERT

...late $3   FRIED PIE

MARROW

Jonathan Kosorek shuttered his popular food truck, Jon's Street Eats, to open a tiny restaurant in 2013 with one concept in mind: whole animal cookery. At Marrow, he brings in one animal at a time, which is raised locally and is natural, organic, and GMO-free. It's an old-fashioned concept that resonates with the chef, who has been cooking for 23 years, many of which were spent in the kitchens of Michelin-starred chefs. "After all," says Jonathan, "we are killing a living animal for our consumption and every step through that process should be respected to its fullest."

Customers line up for Marrow lunches, and scramble for one of the few tables. We suggest "The Deal," which consists of an incredible cheeseburger, "beef fat" fries, and a cold beverage. The heavenly Crispy Potato Salad also beckons, with fried fingerling potatoes, a preserved lemon vinaigrette, arugula, and shaved grana padano.

325 19th Street
510 251 1111
marrowoakland.com

CLASSIC CARS WEST

This is one interesting mash-up. Classic Cars West is a vintage and collectible car showroom as well as an art gallery showcasing artwork from emerging and established Bay Area artists.

Owner Michael Sarcona has a history selling collectible cars. In 2004, he started his business in San Francisco's Mission district. A regular at Oakland's Art Murmur's Saturday Strolls, Michael had passed his current space numerous times while frequenting galleries on the block. When he saw the "for rent" sign on the building, he jumped on it.

Michael's taste in cars is eclectic; he doesn't focus on any one era or make of car. A recent visit to his 8,000 square foot showroom displayed an impressive and wide-ranging assortment, from a sweet pair of 1956 Chryslers (a 300B and New Yorker St. Regis) to a 1963 Jaguar XKE Coupe to a modern classic like the 2008 Aston Martin Vantage V8. One of his favorite cars sold was a 1967 Bizzarrini GT America rumored to have been featured in the opening credits of the movie *Bullitt*.

Michael works with local curators, including Dasha Matsuura and Champagne and Nettles, who fill the gallery each month with talented artists' work. See Classic Cars West's gallery shows at Oakland's First Fridays and Oakland Art Murmur each Saturday, or shop for cars by appointment.

411 26th Street
415 626 1135
classiccarswest.com

XOLO TAQUERIA

Xolo is a nickname for the Mexican hairless dog that Frida Kahlo was so fond of: the Xoloitzcuintli. It's also the popular Uptown Mexican taqueria's mascot. Influential Oakland restaurateur Thomas Schnetz opened this restaurant with Doña Tomás partner Dona Savitsky, as well as Matt Ridgeway (chef at Berkeley's Tacubaya) and Juan Zarate (chef at Doña Tomás) back in 2011, years after he and Dona swore they would never make burritos. "We said, 'Burritos are not Mexican food.' Now we eat our words. We love burritos. So now we make them in our own style along with favorites like tacos and our 'danger dog'. I think, though, that the surf-n-turf burrito is the favorite; grilled carne asada, mojo ajo shrimp with chiles and pintos," admits Tom.

We love Xolo's kitschy feel—bright colors, vintage Mexican matador posters, and black velvet paintings—but don't let it fool you. They take their Mexican taqueria menu seriously and so do their devotees. The sopa de lima, chile relleno burrito, and shrimp tacos keep Oaklanders coming back for more.

1916 Telegraph Avenue
510 986 0151
xolotaqueria.com

DUENDE

Rocco Somazzi opened Duende with chef Paul Canales in a grand 4,000 square foot space with ambitions as high as the restaurant's 25 foot ceilings: to create a space made for experiencing food, drink, art and live music all in one. The Basque-inspired menu is truly a part of former Oliveto chef Paul Canales' make-up, with his father being of Spanish Basque heritage. Careful not to create a culinary experience that's too one-note, his menu is also heavily influenced by the California food scene. Duende's paella is a popular dish and their tapas dishes are inventive and fun.

The loft space above the open kitchen hosts live music from some of the country's most creative artists and the eastern portion of the restaurant is designated "bodega" space, serving as a hip coffee bar in the morning and a sexy wine/cocktail bar at dark.

468 19th Street
510 893 0174
duendeoakland.com

OWLNWOOD

Copenhagen native Rachel Konte is a former design director at Levi's, and spent over 18 years at the company, in both Europe and San Francisco. She combined her years of industry experience with her Danish background for the inspiration behind her women's boutique, OwlNWood. "The owl and the wood both represent the Scandinavian forest and landscape I grew up in, as well as quality and wisdom," she explains.

Rachel sells a combination of new apparel and accessories from small brands alongside vintage finds. The store truly represents her personal style and interests. "It's important to me to help people re-use amazing products and give the products a second life in their closet. The concept of 'timeless' versus 'fashion' is also close to my heart. After 20 years in the fashion industry, I've come to realize that I don't like the way the industry demands us to follow their trends. I like products that can last through time and trends and still be relevant," explains Rachel. OwlNWood shoppers have come to expect an uber-cool and constantly evolving mix of merchandise from this local tastemaker; vintage sweaters next to Swedish-made clogs and locally designed dresses. We also love the infusion of music in her shop. An oversized image of Jimi Hendrix on the back wall draws you in and vintage records from R&B icons create backdrops for displays of pretty little finds like nail polish and jewelry.

45 Grand Avenue
510 579 1439
owlnwood.com

MY MILKSHAKE BRINGS ALL THE BOYS TO THE YARD AND THEY'RE LIKE IT'S BETTER THAN YOURS DAMN RIGHT IT'S BETTER THAN YOURS I COULD TEACH YOU BUT I'D HAVE TO CHARGE

TRUEBURGER

Burger-lovers flock to Trueburger for classic American fast food done right. The Angus beef for their quarter-pound burgers is ground on-site every day. The egg buns are custom made and baked every morning, and their own "secret sauce," a tasty garlic mayo, makes their burgers truly addictive. "Cheeseburger and fries" may be their most popular order, but the menu also offers other entrée options including hot dogs (the Chili-Cheese Dog and Spicy Slaw Dog are especially appealing), a chopped BLT salad, or a bowl of chili. The mushroom burger is a mouth-watering option for vegetarians, and everyone needs to experience their perfectly cooked, thin and crispy French fries. The retro-style menu wouldn't be complete without Trueburger's hand-spun milkshakes and root beer float, both crafted with premium ice cream.

The service is friendly, the 30-seat space is unassuming, and we love the hand painted mural of our fair city, by Lisa Pfeiffer, which pays homage to many of Oakland's landmarks.

146 Grand Avenue
510 208 5678
trueburgeroakland.com

CAFÉ VAN KLEEF

Café Van Kleef officially opened as a bar in 2004, but it feels as though it's been there for decades. Owner and artist Peter Van Kleef built the bar (literally) and decorated the eclectic, artfully cluttered space from artifacts he has collected from his travels around the globe. Vintage hats hang alongside taxidermy animal heads and creepy antique toys. He built it to look like it's over a hundred years old, and most people think it is!

Everyone hangs out at Café Van Kleef. Men in suits sit alongside poets, and local celebrities and politicians hang out with artists, but everyone goes to Van Kleef's to have a drink, meet a friend, or hear live music from the tiny 6x8 foot stage. Most guests opt for what has become Café Van Kleef's iconic cocktail- the Greyhound. Made with freshly squeezed juice and topped with a quarter of a ruby red grapefruit, the bar can easily go through 400 grapefruits in one night.

1621 Telegraph Avenue
510 763 7711
cafevankleef.com

DONUT SAVANT

When co-owner Laurel Davis moved to Oakland three years ago, she set out on a search to find great donuts near home. Frustrated by what she found, she started making the sweet treats out of her kitchen. She experimented with donuts for months until she got to the point when she realized she needed to invest in a donut fryer.

Laurel found her donut fryer on Craigslist; the only catch was that it was that it came with a donut shop. Laurel drove to the shop to check it out, and within a month, she and partner Danielle Feinberg owned not only the donut fryer, but the whole shop. "Rumor has it that our space has been a donut shop for 30+ years. We haven't been able to confirm it, but we're pretty happy with the idea," says Laurel.

Donut Savant specializes in donut holes, and patrons have come to expect the unexpected flavors such as Thai Dust (toasted coconut, ginger, kaffir lime, and roasted chilies) or the Chocolate Bomb (a chocolate donut hole filled with Irish whisky ganache topped with a Guinness and Bailey's glaze). Danielle explains, "We opened Donut Savant because we figured that, like us, our community wanted and in fact deserved, exceptional donuts."

1934 Broadway
510 972 8268
donutsavant.com

TWO JACKS DENIM

When asked what makes his menswear shop unique, Tommy Mierzwinski tells us, "All of our products are made in America. And unlike other shops, our mainstay is denim. We stock brands we believe in, brands with a story, brands not found in department stores. Every product has a story." So does the store itself.

"Two Jacks" refers to two writers with a great influence on Tommy's life—Jack Kerouac and Jack London—both rugged individualists and adventurers who chronicled life in America in two different generations. "Kerouac was from Lowell, MA, and London spent his boyhood in Oakland. I grew up not far from Lowell and I live within walking distance of Heinold's First and Last Chance Saloon, where Jack London was known to have knocked back a few," muses Tommy.

Situated in the historic Packard Lofts building, the feel of Two Jacks Denim is rugged and industrial, with fixtures made by local craftsmen, salvaged wood and vintage furnishings. A vintage typewriter, a *Call of the Wild* movie poster, and scattered photos of his influences allude to the shop's inspiration and ground the space.

2355 Broadway
510 788 5832
twojacksdenim.com

Two Jacks Denim
U.S.-MADE MENSWEAR
FEATURING ARTISANAL DENIM

TELEGRAPH BEER GARDEN

Telegraph Beer Garden's 3,000 square foot outdoor space is filled with picnic tables, old signs, and graffiti. Lots of graffiti. But owner John Mardikian wouldn't have it any other way. "The graffiti has been an ongoing collaboration of countless artists. Some favorites being Gats, Night Owl, Onder, Urban Modernists, Kristi Holoban, and author/illustrator J.Otto Seibold, our longest standing artist," John says.

John tells us that Seibold, the writer and illustrator of beloved children's books like *Olive the Other Reindeer*, has been a fixture at Telegraph Beer Garden since it opened. In honor of his most recent book, *Lost Sloth*, he created a Sloth "shrine" on the beer garden walls, complete with Sloth merchandise, Seibold's books for little ones to enjoy, and of course, his artwork.

The beer garden offers over 80 beers by the bottle and 30 beers on draft. John tells us that the menu has evolved to be what his customers like. "It started out as house-made sausages, but then we started selling natural beef burgers. Pulled pork and green bean sandwiches are a favorite too. Our mac-n-cheese burger came from a customer sarcastically saying that we should serve a slab of grilled macaroni and cheese on top of a burger. We tried it, and it was so yummy we had to put it on the menu."

2318 Telegraph Avenue
510 444 8353
telegraphoakland.com

THE FOX THEATER

Oakland's Fox Theater originally opened in 1928 to 20,000 patrons, eager to hear the Mighty Wurlitzer, take in a live stage show and see one of the new "talkies." The architecture and design, however, may have upstaged the rest with an opulent tiled exterior often referred to as Moorish, Indian, or Baghdadian. The theater was built for a staggering 3.5 million dollars and boasted the largest theater capacity on the west coast at 3,800. Although certainly affected by the Depression, the Fox continued to show first-run movies and double features in the bustling Uptown district until 1965 when the theater closed due to the advent of television and America's changing interests.

In 1978, the theater was purchased by a local couple who went on dates at the theater together in the 1930s. The city purchased the decrepit theater from them in 1996 and Oakland native Phil Tagami made it his mission to see it restored. In 2009, after 28 public hearings and 3 dozen meetings on community outreach, the Fox Theater reopened in all its splendor as a live music venue, drawing crowds from San Francisco for great shows by indie rock and hip hop acts. Today, the theater is once again an Oakland icon and glorious reminder of the city's past.

1807 Telegraph Avenue
510 302 2250
thefoxoakland.com

CHABOT RD

HAWTHORN

RAMEN SHOP

COLLEGE AVE

KEITH AVE

MARKET HALL

MAISON D'ETRE

LAWTON AVE

BELLA VITA

PRETTY PENNY

ATOMIC GARDEN

MANILA AVE

LOOT ANTIQUES

LOST & FOUND

This desirable residential Oakland neighborhood has a shopping district that has always drawn crowds. Charming boutiques line the streets, as do artisan food markets and enticing restaurants.

ATOMIC GARDEN

This heavenly bohemian emporium stocks a wide array of handcrafted finds: home/kitchen ware, women's apparel, accessories, baby/children's gifts, bath/beauty products, and paper/craft supplies. Their selection might be vast, but each and every item that is brought into the store is there for a reason. Owners Jamie Kidson and Adrienne Armstrong carefully choose items that are not only pleasing to the eye, but also made thoughtfully. Most items are either made locally, sustainably produced, or benefitting a greater good. "It's not a prerequisite, but I think Adrienne and I are drawn to items that are good for the earth, have a story behind them or are made by hand," says Jamie. Globally-inspired Dosa dresses mingle with hand-carved rolling pins made from local fallen trees and Atomic Garden-branded sweet-smelling soaps and balms. They have developed quite a following for their essential oil-based body care line, which includes handmade goat's milk soaps and balms for the hands, lips and body. Their newest addition is AG Scent No. 1, their go at bottling the intoxicating scent of the shop itself, which is a blend of vetiver, clary sage, geranium, fennel, and cyprus organic oils.

5453 College Avenue
510 923 0543
atomicgardenoakland.com

HAWTHORN

Hawthorn *could* be the type of boutique that intimidates shoppers. The salesgirls are impossibly cool, the bohemian space is spare and chic, and the racks are filled with blouses, dresses, and jeans from local and indie designers. But it's not. Owner Laurie Lion is the kind of woman who really looks into your eyes when you speak and laughs at the drop of a hat. She calls you "babe" in the most endearing way and knows just what you need in your closet.

The boutique is one of the most popular women's boutiques in the city and Laurie is proud to sell clothing and accessories from Bay Area designers like Curator, Ali Golden, Marisa Haskell, The Podolls, and Sarah Swell. "We're really lucky to have so many incredible designers in the Bay Area, and carrying local designers allows us to follow two of our ethos: building community and sustainability. We feel it's important to know where your garment was made, by who and how. With so many creative folks in the area who also share our aesthetic we can accomplish this without sacrificing our love for fashion and remain true to our style," says Laurie.

5854 College Avenue
510 594 8380
hawthornboutique.com

N.01
BELLOCQ
BREAKFAST
Black Tea Blend

ORGANIC

TESTER

N.31-13
SIAM BASIL
LEMONGRASS
Herbal Blend

ORGANIC

TESTER

N.47
THE QUEEN'S
GUARD
Black Tea and Floral Blend

ORGANIC

TESTER

N.20
KIKUYA
Green Tea and Rose Blend

ORGANIC

TESTER

N.39
HINDU HOLIDAY
Rooibos Blend

ORGANIC

TESTER

BEYOND BACON

KINFOLK

OTTOLENGHI

MAISON D'ETRE

Maison d'Etre is 1,600 square feet of covetable gifts and amazing finds for the home. Owners Patty Brunn and Fred Womack's impressive array of goods include: table linens, cookbooks, children's books and gifts, soaps and lotions, bedding, candles, jewelry, and stationery... and the list goes on and on.

The store is a feast for the senses; vintage armoires hold stacks of charming linens, shelves display light-catching glassware and vintage chandeliers dangle from the ceiling. Every nook and cranny is filled with pretty things begging to be taken home.

Maison d'Etre attracts a diverse group of customers and is a Rockridge institution. Oaklanders of 23 years, Patty and Fred sum up the people of this city beautifully: "Uphill swimmers, Oaklanders have a great spirit expressed in great businesses, great food, and other creative endeavors. Oakland's got a big heart, always thriving, like a salmon making its way upstream, to be a better city."

5640 College Avenue
510 658 2801
maisondetre.com

MARKET HALL

Eager to give Oaklanders an alternative to big box grocery store shopping, retail pioneers (and siblings) Sara, Peter and Tony Wilson opened Market Hall back in 1986. The European style market is a collection of Market Hall-owned shops and meticulously chosen vendors, including The Pasta Shop, Paul Marcus Wines, Highwire Coffee Roasters, Market Hall Bakery, The Flower & The B, Hapuku Fish Shop, Marin Sun Farms Butcher Shop, and Market Hall Produce. Oakland's Oliveto restaurant, a breeding-ground for some of the area's best chefs, fills the corner spot and anchors the space. Market Hall offers everything you need from a daily market under one roof; fresh meats, cheeses, seafood, produce, wine and fresh flowers. Of course, this is Oakland, so quality is of utmost importance.

Loads of locals make Highwire Coffee Roasters a part of their morning ritual. The Pasta Shop sells fresh pasta, sure, but shoppers also go crazy over their cheese counter, specialty groceries and prepared foods. Market Hall Bakery is hard to resist, offering scrumptious, freshly baked pastries, breads, cookies, and cakes, and Market Hall Produce offers an excellent selection of organic and locally grown fruits and veggies. Paul Marcus Wines focuses on Californian and European wines, with most bottles selling for $6 to $25, for

your everyday drinking pleasure. Stop by Marin Sun Farms Butcher Shop for locally raised, grass-fed beef, lamb, and goat, as well as pasture-raised chicken and pork. Customers love The Flower & The B for their amazing selection of flowers, and the team at Hapuku Fish Shop really cares about sustainability, striving to help customers make the very best choices when buying their seafood.

5655 College Avenue
510 250 6000
rockridgemarkethall.com

BELLA VITA

After working for Gap Inc. for 17 years, Jennifer Viale found her calling. In 2000, she opened her charming shop in Rockridge, and 14 years later moved into a space almost twice its size, just down the street. The current 1,400 square-foot space is chock full of treasures including women's apparel, accessories and gifts for child and baby. But it wasn't always that way. Jennifer tells us, "When I first started Bella Vita, my focus was on vintage finds. I didn't sell any clothing or children's items. When my daughter was born, I decided to add children's items to the shop, and focus on local and indie designers. I still have a touch of vintage in the shop though, and a lot of the new products I sell have a vintage feel to them."

"My customer is someone looking for something unique. She doesn't want what everybody else has. She loves that she doesn't know what quite what to expect at Bella Vita; it's always changing," explains Jennifer. What hasn't changed is her dedication to supporting local Bay Area makers, including Cookie and the Dude, Giddy Giddy, Rikshaw Design, Good on Paper, Ses Petites Mains, Whitney Smith, and Carmela Rose.

5511 College Avenue
510 653 1639
bellavitahome.com

LOOT ANTIQUES

Loot Antiques owner Ron Morgan loves the thrill of the hunt. He regularly shops estate sales, flea markets, and consignment shops. So often, in fact, that he had to open a shop to keep his collections "fluid." Constantly asked where he finds his wares, Ron would answer, "I won't tell you where, but I found some good loot," and the name of the shop was born.

Loot specializes in antique and reproduction furniture and home décor items, as well as new items. Think antique furniture, candles, and pretty little trinkets. Ron is also a celebrated floral designer, and often his arrangements are artfully scattered throughout the space. Ron's beautifully eclectic assortment is currently housed in a 1,600 square-foot space with a warm afternoon glow that matches the no-pressure attitude you're greeted with at the door.

5391 College Avenue
510 547 1400
lootantiques.com

RAMEN SHOP

Jerry Jaksich, Rayneil De Guzman and Sam White met while working together at Chez Panisse. Sam tells us, "We would all talk at Chez Panisse about ramen. We had each been to Japan and were on a desperate search for the perfect bowl in the East Bay. We just kept coming back to the question, 'What if we made ramen with good ingredients?' Handmade noodles with stuff from local farmers." They brought their dream to life in 2013 when they opened Ramen Shop in Oakland's Rockridge neighborhood.

The menu at Ramen Shop is small and changes daily. "It's a reflection of what is available from our farmer friends," says Sam. "We always have a plate of house-made pickles. There is always a fried rice, and we have three ramens, one of which is 100% vegetarian."

When they open their doors for dinner in the evening, throngs of patrons rush through the doors, eager to enjoy a good bowl of noodles. "Ramen is the great equalizer," says Sam. "Little kids like their noodles and so do their grandparents."

5812 College Avenue
510.788.6370
ramenshop.com

LOST & FOUND

Lost & Found was born out of a late-night conversation among good friends Alison McLennan, Brooke Livingston and Erik Whitaker. Their collective love of quality vintage items, restoration and modern design were combined into their eclectic business model; a shop selling a mix of vintage home décor and furniture, upcycled vintage items, and goods made by local artists.

The three friends opened Lost & Found in 2013 in a free-standing 1,200 square-foot space in Oakland's Rockridge district. Like the wares they sell, the space has an interesting past; it was formerly used as an auto body shop, pet supply store, mattress showroom, and Obama call center.

Their multi-faceted assortment often strikes a sentimental chord. "Our customers love coming in and seeing things they grew up with or that their grandmother had. They also love the candles, oddities and art that we carry," says Brooke.

5357 College Avenue
510 858 5011
lostandfoundstore.us

PRETTY PENNY

Before she opened her vintage boutique, owner Sarah Dunbar set up shop in her one-bedroom apartment once a month to sell vintage clothing to friends while serving drinks and snacks. Her pop-up became so popular she needed to open a shop to meet the demand, and Pretty Penny was born.

Her boutique carries vintage clothing and accessories for men and women, and is known among seasoned vintage aficionados for carrying a well-edited selection of women's dresses, sunglasses and jewelry. The top floor is a vintage shoe-lover's heaven, meticulously organized by color. "In addition to vintage, we also sell a few select small designers of clothing and jewelry," says Sarah.

The community is very important to Sarah, who has lived in Oakland for 15 years. "We often donate to local organizations, and we have let people use the space for fundraisers and sponsored local events. And of course, we shop locally."

5488 College Avenue
510 594 9219
prettypennyclothing.com

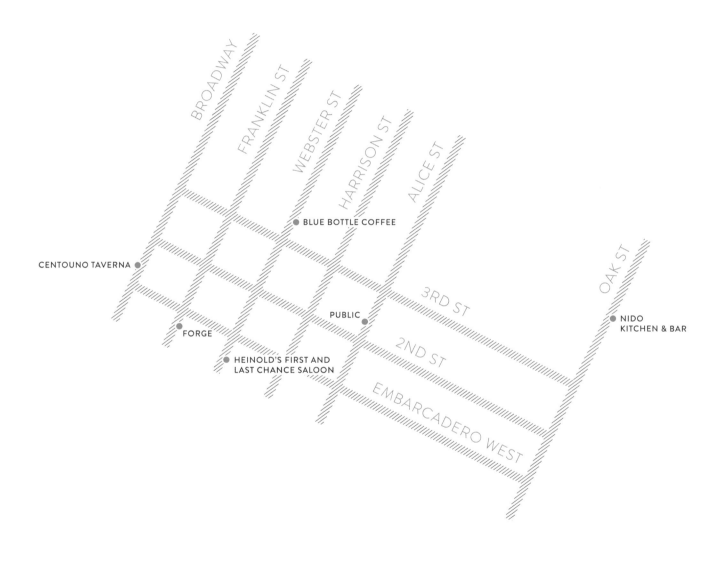

Step back in time at Heinold's First and Last Chance Saloon, where author Jack London hung out and drafted notes for his novels. Named after the author, who spent his boyhood in Oakland, this seaport neighborhood retains its unique industrial, warehouse feel, and is in an exciting state of growth.

NIDO KITCHEN & BAR

"Nido" translates to "nest" in Spanish, and owners Silvia and Cory McCollow strove to create just that when they created their restaurant in the industrial Jack London district where they also live. "We incorporated building materials from the local area, shipping containers from the waterfront, pallets from the produce mart, old construction sign posts, etc, to help an interesting aesthetic to the space...just as a bird builds its nest from things found in the area," explains Silvia.

Silvia is Nido's chef, and her influences span Mexico's central and Pacific coast. She pulls from family recipes for the menu, which includes small and large plates and change seasonally. "We source our meats from producers who raise their animals humanely with no growth hormones or antibiotics. We love California's produce, so there are many vegetable-oriented dishes on our menu as well," she says.

Silvia and Cory are also particular about the ingredients used in the cocktails served at Nido. "We strive to use spirits from small distilleries who have traceable and sustainable practices. This is often seen with food, but not as often with cocktails," says Silvia.

444 Oak Street
510 444 6436
nidooakland.com

BLUE BOTTLE COFFEE

James Freeman started Blue Bottle in 2002 in a tiny space behind Temescal's Doña Tomás, and in 2009 moved the business into a 7,500 square foot space in the Jack London district. The vast headquarters holds offices, a roastery, pastry kitchen, lab, cupping room and 400 square-foot retail space. "I fall in love with buildings, and the moment I walked into our Webster Street space, I knew I wanted to make Blue Bottle headquarters here. The light, the proportions, the honest materials... they all conspired to make me want to be here," laughs James.

Blue Bottle has a near fanatical following, perhaps due to the fact that James made a vow to, "only sell coffee less than 48 hours out of the roaster to my customers, so they may enjoy coffee at its peak of flavor. I will only use the finest organic, and pesticide-free, shade-grown beans." Today Oakland-grown Blue Bottle has cafes in the San Francisco Bay Area and New York City.

300 Webster Street
510 653 3394
bluebottlecoffee.com

PUBLIC

San Francisco-based Public opened their Oakland warehouse and store in 2012. They not only store and ship Public bikes and gear from this location, but also assemble bikes to ship to customers nationwide.

Public is the brainchild of design fanatic Rob Forbes, founder of Design Within Reach. Sure, Public bikes ride as smooth as silk through the city streets, but they also appeal to riders' aesthetics. Available in a rainbow of chic color options, the bikes have classic Dutch-inspired styling, which translates to a "step-through" model, which is well-suited to riders wearing skirts, many of which prefer not to swing a leg over a typical frame crossbar. And of course, there are clever accessories, including charming baskets, retro bells, and cool helmets.

Don't let their stylishness fool you, though. Public bikes are made for everyone: the everyday bicyclist who regularly rides to work and around town, the occasional rider taking their bike to the farmer's market, and the newbie who is buying an adult bike for the first time and wants to recapture the joy they felt as a kid. Step into the shop and smile.

205 Alice Street
510 251 1581
publicbikes.com

FORGE

Soak in the waterfront view at this Jack London Square destination and devour a handcrafted Neapolitan-style pizza and artisanal beer or house-made tonic on tap. Forge, whose name refers to a hearth used to bake items at very hot temperatures, features wood-fired cooking, and the Italian Valoriani oven definitely takes center stage. In addition to pizzas, popular items include cheese curds, house made pickles, and chicken potpie.

Owned by restaurateurs Bob Burke and Michael Karp and designed by architect/builder Andy Byrnes, the eatery boasts over 4,000 square feet, which manages to feel warm and cozy despite its size. "We chose Jack London Square as the home for our first restaurant because we love the waterfront location and the 'rustic' feel of the space for Forge," said Karp. We adore the outdoor seating, which features fire pits to keep customers cozy in the chilly months, and offers gorgeous sunset views all year long.

66 Franklin Street
510 268 3200
theforgepizza.com

HEINOLD'S FIRST AND LAST CHANCE SALOON

Believe the lore, this circa 1883 watering hole is the real deal. Jack London studied and made notes for his novels sitting at these tables, Robert Louis Stevenson knocked back a few while waiting for his ship to be outfitted for his final trip to Samoa, and Oakland mayor John L. Davie brought President Taft in for a cold one.

Heinold's First and Last Chance Saloon opened right where it currently stands, near the water at the foot of Webster Street, over 130 years ago. Johnny Heinold paid $100 for the then-bunk house, named it J.M. Heinold's Saloon, and transformed it into a saloon catering to the men coming in and out of the port. In the '20s, a ferry bringing passengers between Oakland and Alameda docked right next to Heinold's. As Alameda was a "dry" town at the time, it was truly the "first and last chance" for refreshments of the alcoholic sort. The nickname stuck and became the saloon's official name.

Today, stepping down into this dimly lit bar is like stepping back in time. Very little has changed; Heinold's still uses the original gas lights (and is the only business in California to do so), and on the wall hangs the clock that ticked its final tock during the 1906 earthquake. The floors, which were thrown off during the quake, feel reminiscent of a fun house, and many original relics fill the space, including the stove, lanterns, tables, and the old bar rail.

48 Webster Street
510 839 6761
heinolds.com

CENTOUNO TAVERNA

The rustic Italian menu at Centouno Taverna is an homage to chef/owner Fabio Dalle Vacche's mother who owned a restaurant outside of Parma, Italy for over 40 years. As Fabio says, "The food was simple yet delicious. Fresh and natural ingredients make for dishes that are full of flavor." "Mamma" comes to the restaurant frequently, to make sure the food tastes the way it should and is cooked to perfection. Fabio didn't just borrow from his mother's recipe box; he also imported the antique wooden tables and wine barrels from her Italian restaurant.

One of Centouno's most popular dishes is the Torta Frita con Salumi, a puffed dough, fried until light golden brown, served alongside a variety of cured meats. Fabio explains that in Italy, torta frita is not typically a restaurant dish, but rather a family specialty; each family has their own take on the dish. Mamma's is so delicious, so *perfect*, that the recipe is a carefully guarded secret; only Fabio, his wife and Mamma know the recipe. We also suggest their mouthwatering osso bucco and any of the fresh pastas.

101 Broadway
510 433 5030
centouno101.com

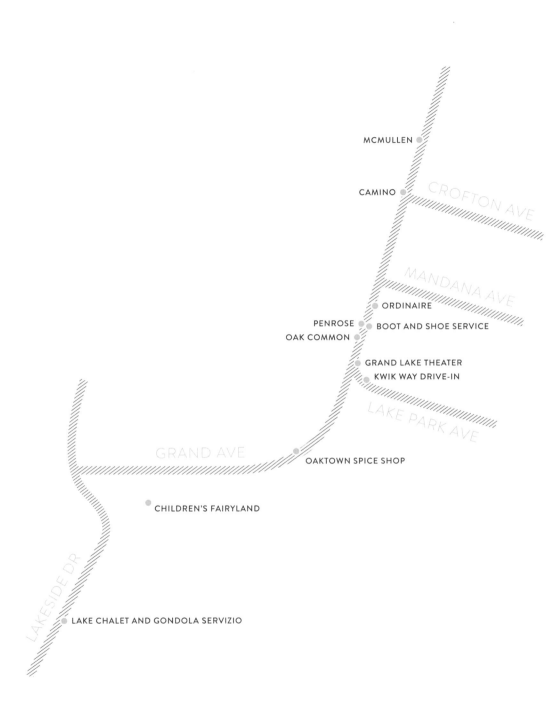

MCMULLEN

CAMINO

CROFTON AVE

MANDANA AVE

ORDINAIRE

PENROSE   BOOT AND SHOE SERVICE
OAK COMMON

GRAND LAKE THEATER
KWIK WAY DRIVE-IN

LAKE PARK AVE

GRAND AVE

OAKTOWN SPICE SHOP

CHILDREN'S FAIRYLAND

LAKESIDE DR

LAKE CHALET AND GONDOLA SERVIZIO

GRAND LAKE & LAKE MERRITT

HIMALAYAN PINK
COARSE SALT
1/8 oz bag * 1 oz bag
$1.00 * $2.00

The neighborhood by picturesque Lake Merritt boasts both longtime favorites—the Grand Lake Theater, one of the city's best farmer's markets, the retro-appeal of Children's Fairyland—and, increasingly, trendy restaurants and shops.

ORDINAIRE

Owner Bradford Taylor tell us, "Ordinaire refers to 'vin ordinaire' or 'everyday wine,' which is the wine that the French winemaker never puts in the bottle, but instead holds back for family, close friends and the local bistro. I want my shop to be a place where people think of wine as an everyday beverage, not as a luxury good."

While living in France, Bradford learned to love French wine as well as French wine culture. "In Paris, shopkeepers and consumers are passionate about French wine, and there is a tight network between winemakers and the people consuming that wine. I wanted to create a space that fostered similar interactions, so I focus heavily on California wines."

Bradford chooses wines from small producers making wine with natural methods from France, Italy and Germany. He follows the common French practice of writing the price right on the wine bottle, and likes the idea of a $15 bottle rubbing shoulders with a $85 bottle of wine. "The notion of 'top-shelf' is nonsense," he states. While Ordinaire does have some wines at the high and low ends of the spectrum, most bottles range from $18 to $28.

3354 Grand Avenue
510 629 3944
ordinairewine.com

OAK COMMON

Jeffrey Pobart and David Yun opened Oak Common in 2012, after moving from San Francisco in 2009. Their 1,260 square foot space is located across from the historic Grand Lake Theater.

Jeffrey tells us, "We have put together a collection of brands that we describe as 'a refined interpretation of current trends,' but we always make sure that we keep the unique perspective of Oaklanders in mind." And that's not just "shop talk." Jeffrey really listens to the men and women who shop in his store. "There is something to be said for taking the time to learn who your customers are. We spent time getting to know our customers when we opened; listening to what brands and types of goods they wanted, and what the neighborhood was currently lacking," he says. "Of course, when we bring in new brands it is always within our own aesthetic tastes as well, but it's been a successful and symbiotic relationship thus far."

Jeffrey and David connect with the community in an unexpected way; they also run a fine arts project space in the part of the store called Backstock Gallery, with monthly installations. With a focus on film/video, installation, and experimental forms of art, Jeffrey and David provide artists with a venue for showing their work in these often under-represented genres.

3231 Grand Avenue
510 285 6629
oakcommon.com

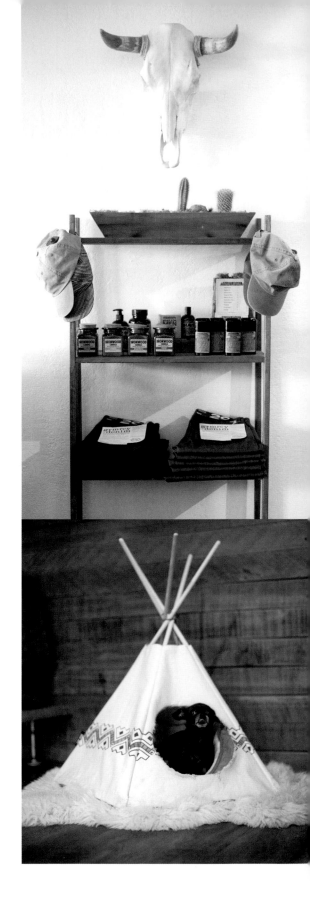

CAMINO

At 5,000 square feet with 15-foot ceilings, Camino is vast, yet the space feels warm, rustic and cozy. We assume it's the combination of the 30-feet long tables, set with vintage prayer chairs and the iron chandeliers laced with delicate bay leaves and outfitted with paper lanterns that give off a soft glow. Add the bonus of the crackling fire in the open kitchen, and Camino's atmosphere makes the restaurant one of the city's most charming spaces.

The warmth and flicker of the flames are undoubtedly romantic, but they aren't for show. Chef Russell Moore cooks most everything on the menu by fire. The former Chez Panisse chef explains, "That self-imposed limitation forces creativity..." Business partner and wife Allison Hopelain adds, "We have a small menu that changes every day, and while people love our Dungeness crab, grilled kebabs, and roasted duck consommé, we are also kind of known for our vegetarian dishes. We sneak a lot of vegetables into the meat and fish dishes. We take advantage of Russ' years developing relationships with local farmers to get great produce."

3917 Grand Avenue
510 547 5035
caminorestaurant.com

OAKTOWN SPICE SHOP

John Beaver got his start in spices as a teenager. "I got a 'spice apprenticeship' in a shop in Milwaukee. I got really into spices early on, and I think they just became part of my physiological make up from inhaling them all day long! I might be 97% spice," laughs John. "One won't know until they do a postmortem autopsy on me."

John owns the shop with wife Erica Perez. They sell top quality herbs, spices and hand-mixed blends to locals, as well as customers who travel to shop in their emporium. John tells us that, "Some of them love to create, to cook and to eat, and others are looking for interesting gifts for those in their lives that like to create, cook and eat." Customers love their vast selection of salts, including the enticing Cyprus Citron Lemon Flake Sea Salt. Their most popular spice blends include their Better Than Everything Bagel Spice and Persian Lime Curry Rub, and they take pride in selling spices that are often hard to find in the states, such as barberries, black limes and sumac.

530 Grand Avenue
510 201 5400
oaktownspiceshop.com

GRAND LAKE THEATER

Grand Lake Theater has been the pride Oakland for years and has anchored the Grand Lake district since the Twenties. Allen Michaan took over the theater, an architectural gem just north of Lake Merritt, back in 1979 with one mission: to keep classic movie theaters such as this one alive in an age of multiplexes and commercialism. He spent over $4 million revitalizing the circa 1926 theater, and went to great lengths to keep the classic art deco ornamentation intact while adding a 2nd screen in the vast balcony. In 1985, he added two additional screens, acquired from former storefront spaces that were adjacent to the theater.

Most important to Allen is preserving the classic movie-going experience. On Friday and Saturday nights, the 52 x 72 foot illuminated rooftop sign with 2,800 light bulbs lights up the Oakland sky. Once patrons are seated, an organist rises from the floor playing the Mighty Wurlitzer organ for a brief pre-show concert. Allen tells us, "The Grand Lake Theater is a special survivor of the movie palace era. Today the movie-going experience has been cheapened. This theater has a special place in my heart and I want to keep it alive as long as I can." Moviegoers at the Grand Lake don't have to sit through obnoxious commercials or deal with the flashing lights and noise of arcade games outside the theaters. Real butter tops their popcorn and you get the feeling that all of the staff really wants to be there. But then, who wouldn't?

3200 Grand Avenue
510 452 3556
renaissancerialto.com

LAKE CHALET AND GONDOLA SERVIZIO

Lake Chalet is the place to go for picturesque dining on the lake. Originally built in 1909 as a pumping station for the Oakland Fire Department, the building was added to four years later to create the Lake Merritt Boathouse. The facilities included locker rooms, a tea room, and restaurants and was the launching spot for regattas and boat excursions on the lake. In 2009, owners Gar and Lara Truppelli brought the historic space back to life as Lake Chalet, a restaurant featuring a gorgeous 80 foot long marble bar overlooking the water, ample outdoor seating (right on the water) and a warm-weather outdoor bar, as well as an elegant dining room and private dining space. Customers love their raw bar, fresh seafood entrees and expertly mixed cocktails.

For a perfectly romantic night on Lake Merritt, we suggest reserving a ride with Gondola Servizio, an authentic Venetian gondola service, with tours departing daily out of Lake Chalet. Owners Angelino Sandri and April Quinn shipped their gorgeous, handmade Venetian gondolas directly from the "city of love" to the shores of Lake Merritt, and their gondoliers are the real deal. Trained in Italy, they handle the boats with the finesse of an artist and true Italian charm.

1520 Lakeside Drive
510 208 5253
thelakechalet.com

MCMULLEN

Sherri McMullen's job has its perks. For one, she travels to New York and Paris four to six times a year to buy for her self-named stylish, high-end women's boutique. But don't let the travel fool you; Sherri works hard at keeping her customers dressed to the nines.

She opened in her first boutique just blocks away from the current shop in 2007, and has always found it imperative to source covetable clothing and accessories from designers not often found in the Bay Area. "My goal, when opening McMullen, was to provide women with clothing and accessories that help them feel confident and beautiful. Our clients have been shopping with us for years now, and often times 2 to 3 generations from a single family shop with us. I love that I can provide something for women at every age," explains Sherri. "I try to keep a tightly edited assortment so that my customers aren't overwhelmed, and I always think about my clients when I buy," she says.

Known for carrying emerging, unique designers, McMullen stocks Suno, Rhie, Veronica Beard, Jenni Kayne, and Carven. Giving back to the community is important to Sherri, and she often hosts charity events benefiting organizations that empower women and children.

1235 Grand Avenue
510 658 6906
shopmcmullen.com

BOOT AND SHOE SERVICE

Charlie Hallowell opened Boot and Shoe Service in late 2009, following the success of his restaurant Pizzaiolo in Temescal. Housed in—surprise!—a former shoe repair shop just a block from the Grand Lake Theater, the restaurant helped revitalize the neighborhood. Like his first venture, the menu is based around his superb pizzas, which again hail from a wood burning pizza oven, but also includes a variety of dishes inspired by what's fresh and what's local. The warm, intimate space features an open kitchen and a sexy bar at the back of the restaurant. Well-crafted cocktails make a wait at the bar time well spent.

Two years after opening, Charlie took over the neighboring space and expanded the restaurant, making breakfast and lunch service possible. What was once just a dinner destination became a popular weekend brunch spot and a daytime hangout for locals, complete with a large communal table and stools and a narrow bar lining the exposed brick walls. Boot and Shoe's sunny back patio is a perfect spot to spend the morning with a cappuccino and perfectly flaky, warm-from-the-oven croissant over the morning paper.

3308 Grand Avenue
510 763 2668
bootandshoeservice.com

KWIK WAY DRIVE-IN

Kwik Way Drive-In's glorious retro architecture and iconic signage was brought back to life in 2011 by restaurateur Gary Rizzo, who is passionate about seeing the Oakland institution regain the glory it had in the '50s and '60s. The classic Grand Lake drive-in served burgers, fries, apple pie and malted milk shakes to Oakland families back in the day, and today it serves all that, and more.

Gary has created an extensive diner-style menu that includes rotisserie chicken, sandwiches, burgers, soup, classic sides, and homemade strawberry shortcake; all of it made on the premises. Beef is ground on-site, buns and garlic mayo are made fresh each day, and even their ice cream sandwiches are handmade at the drive-in. You can taste the heart that Gary has put into revitalizing this iconic spot, which is a perfect place for a quick meal before catching a movie at the neighboring Grand Lake Theater or setting off for walk around Lake Merritt.

500 Lake Park Avenue
510 832 1300
kwikwaydrivein.com

PENROSE

The glass canopy fanning out over the open kitchen at Penrose feels reminiscent of the canopies that jut out over the classic Paris Metro station entryways. And, like a great Parisian spot, chef/owner Charlie Hallowell has created a restaurant that is at once neighborhood-y, scene-y, and a place to enjoy a top-notch meal. Much of the menu is cooked in the fire, and is described by Charlie as being, "very elemental and inspired by many different cultures and regions." The menu changes daily, but their grilled rib eye with uni butter and tarragon, oysters on the half-shell and flatbreads are mainstays.

The size of the bar makes it apparent that cocktails are not just an afterthought at Penrose. It spans the entire south side of the restaurant. Cate Whalen oversees the bar and her cocktails are perfectly balanced and beautifully crafted, making the bar just as much a destination as the restaurant itself.

3311 Grand Avenue
510-444-1649
penroseoakland.com

CHILDREN'S FAIRYLAND

In 1948, Oakland businessman Arthur Navlet approached the Lake Merritt Breakfast Club—an organization dedicated to the betterment of the lake and surrounding city—with his plans for a storybook theme park, featuring charming fairy tale sets, as well as farm animals and live entertainment. The group loved the idea and with the support of Oakland Parks Department, raised $50,000 to see Navlet's dream become a reality.

Situated on the shores of Lake Merritt, the park opened to the children of Oakland in 1950, when admission ranged from 9 to 14 cents and costumed fairy tale characters led children and their parents through the park. Puppet shows, kid-size rides (including the popular Jolly Trolly train), friendly animals, and over 35 interactive sets that brought children into their favorite stories and fairy tales kept families entertained. Despite all that, it's the Fairyland "magic key" that has captured the imaginations of children for decades. When inserted in one of the many audio boxes throughout the park the holder is rewarded with a classic fairy tale.

Today, the park, which was restored in the 1990s, retains its charm and appeal. Fairyland still attracts throngs of children and their parents, and the magic keys—which come in every color of the rainbow—remain an iconic symbol of Fairyland and of the city itself.

699 Bellevue Avenue
510 452 2259
fairyland.org

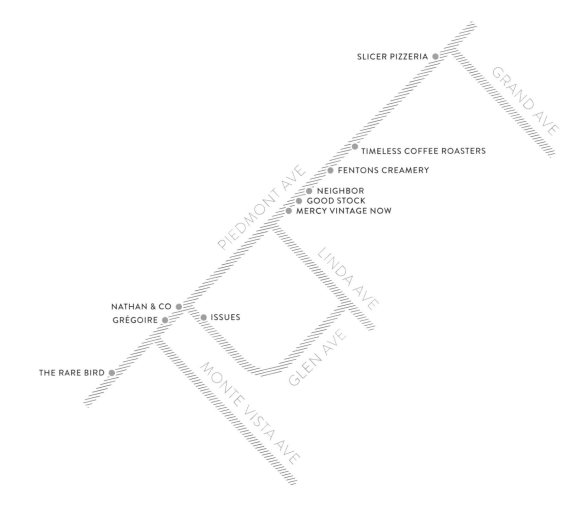

SLICER PIZZERIA

TIMELESS COFFEE ROASTERS

FENTONS CREAMERY

NEIGHBOR

GOOD STOCK

MERCY VINTAGE NOW

GRAND AVE

PIEDMONT AVE

LINDA AVE

NATHAN & CO

GRÉGOIRE

ISSUES

GLEN AVE

THE RARE BIRD

MONTE VISTA AVE

THIS IS

PIEDMONT AVENUE

Lovely tree-lined Piedmont Avenue has been a shopping destination for almost a hundred years, and it seems to just get better with age. Stroll the avenue and grab a bite to eat in one of the 'hood's many tempting eateries or drop some cash in its indie boutiques.

MERCY VINTAGE NOW

Owners Karen Anderson and Jenny Velte did not expect the reception they received from Piedmont Avenue shoppers when they opened their vintage clothing store in 2009. "We cried at the end of our first day of business. We nearly sold out of clothes and had no idea what we were going to sell the next day," laughs Karen.

They were attracted to the charming and popular neighborhood due to its proximity to East Bay institutions Piedmont Theatre and Fentons Creamery, but quickly found it was also an incredibly supportive and welcoming neighborhood. "We literally had cheers of encouragement from passers-by as we were rehabbing the store before we opened," they explain.

The shop is consistently listed as one of the best vintage shops in the Bay Area and the men and women who shop there know to come often, as they replenish their stock on a regular basis. "We're inspired by the hunt for amazing clothes," Jenny says. "Trends may come and go, but good style is inspiring."

"We are both lifelong thrifters, brought up by mothers who didn't know the meaning of buying new," she adds. "The love of vintage clothing brought us together. We're kindred spirits."

4188 Piedmont Avenue
510 654 5599
mercyvintage.com

FENTONS CREAMERY

In 1894, E.S. Fenton founded Fentons Creamery in the city of Oakland. E.S. loved kids so much so that he had thirteen of them, and they all took part in the family business. Melvin Fenton, E.S.'s grandson, is credited for persuading his grandfather to produce ice cream when he was a young boy. The family added the restaurant and soda fountain in 1922, and moved into their current Piedmont Avenue space in 1961.

Melvin grew up to become an ice cream maker for the family business, and along with Fentons candy maker George Farren, invented Rocky Road ice cream, its name acknowledging the hardships of the Great Depression. Today, the ice cream parlor sells over a ton of ice cream a day, all made on premises. "We say, 'from the cow to you in 5 days or less,' and that's what we deliver!" says Nini Curry Whidden, who with husband (and ice cream maker) Gregory Scott Whidden, currently owns the business.

Fentons creates a variety of desserts including frozen yogurt, sorbet, ice cream cakes and pies and their own brand of candy, Myrtle's Munchies, added in 2012. Fentons' most popular dishes and confections are their signature Black and Tan sundae, their caramel sauce (sold by the jar as well), and their classic crab salad sandwich. Nini observes, "What is most wonderful about Fentons is that it's a place where you find a cross section of the entire community; senior citizens, EMT's or firefighters in for a quick bite, or a big family gathering for a birthday... teens, college kids, weekly meetings of moms with

newborns. We've had 70 year wedding anniversaries and onsite engagements!"

After stuffing yourself silly on ice cream, make sure to swing by their gift shop Myrtle's Lodge (it's right across the street) to shop for old time candies, retro kiddie toys and Fentons Creamery paraphernalia, including glassware, baseball caps and tees.

4226 Piedmont Avenue
510 658 7000
fentonscreamery.com

GRÉGOIRE

In response to the lack of high-end French take-out in the area, Grégoire owners Tara and Grégoire Jacquet opened their tiny Piedmont Avenue restaurant in 2002. The menu changes monthly, but customers will always find classically trained French chef Grégoire Jacquet's addictive potato puffs. They have inspired many copycats, but none can match his puffs with crispy exterior and melt-in-your-mouth bite. Grégoire explains, "They were inspired by something I ate while growing up in France, but they're completely original. What makes them work is not just the batter, but how we cook them. I even brought in special equipment to make sure they're not bruised while we're frying them."

When asked why he chose to open a take-out spot versus a restaurant, the chef tells us, "Because people are busy, and they don't always have the time to go to a sit-down restaurant to get good food. My food is just like the food you would find in a fine restaurant, but put in a box. The only thing missing is a big room out front, and waiters."

Using French cooking techniques with quality ingredients, Grégoire serves all entrees and sandwiches in his charming and unmistakable corrugated octagonal box with checkerboard paper.

4001 Piedmont Avenue
510 547 3444
gregoirerestaurant.com

ISSUES

In early 2007, owners Joe Colley and Noella Teele found themselves searching for a copy of a magazine that featured Joe (who is also a sound artist) and couldn't find it anywhere. It was at that moment that the idea for Issues hit them: Why not open a magazine shop? "It just seemed like the perfect idea, as there were no stores in the area that focused on magazines, and an available space on our block," they say. "We joke about it now... Right as print was starting to die, we decide to open a store specializing in it."

It's no joke, however, that Joe and Noella seem to have the perfect backgrounds for the business. In the '90s, Joe worked for Tower Records, when it was the place to buy obscure magazines from all over the world. The experience he gained working for the retail giant, as well as his time working at a newsstand in San Francisco's Union Square, have served him well. Noella spent the '90s managing record stores and that experience helps her keep Issues ticking.

Issues is one of those shops that makes you feel a little bit cooler for having discovered it. Every wall in the store is filled with their comprehensive collection of international and domestic magazines on all subjects, from fashion to food to biking to music. There are stacks of magazines piled up in the center of the room as well, and on the periphery are some handpicked records, t-shirts, pens, books and some seriously amazing zines.

20 Glen Avenue
510 652 5700
issuesshop.com

TIMELESS COFFEE ROASTERS

Timeless Coffee Roasters is a charming coffee roaster/coffee bar/vegan bakery and is the brainchild of RJ Leimpeter. RJ is a former head roaster for San Francisco's popular coffee brand Sightglass and dreamt of opening the business for years. RJ tells us that he chose the north end of the avenue—where he has lived for the past ten years—as it was quieter and didn't have many places to grab a bite and a great cup of freshly roasted coffee. He teamed up with Violett Slocum, a vegan pastry maker and chocolatier extraordinaire to bring her picture-perfect treats to the menu, and Timeless opened in late 2012.

This neighborhood spot quickly gained cult-status among Oaklanders—vegan or not—and rightfully so. Violett's chocolates, cookies, biscotti, carrot cake, and Hostess-inspired baked goods are not only easy on the eyes, but are truly mouth-watering. If sweets aren't your thing, stop by and grab a vegan "beef" potpie or mac-n-"cheese" for lunch or hang out over brunch and savor the "chicken" and waffles and one of the best cups of coffee in Oakland.

4252 Piedmont Avenue
510 985 1360
timelesscoffeeroasters.com

THE RARE BIRD

Stop into The Rare Bird, and you'll find the work of over 100 local designers and artists. Owner Erica Skone-Rees explains, "Our clientele is diverse. They may range in age from 20 to 80, but what unites them is their dedication to supporting local businesses and appreciation of locally created goods."

Erica curates a collection of art, home wares, vintage items, clothing and accessories that makes shopping fun. On the side, Erica designs a jewelry line, Metaphor, which she also sells in the shop. And somehow she also finds time to paint, build terrariums, do ceramic work, sew and collage.

"Aside from our vast collection of locally created art and goods, what makes us special is our personal connection to the community," Erica says. "We genuinely care about our clients and artists, and that translates to our relationships with them." In 2011, she spearheaded the creation of Third Thursdays Piedmont Avenue Stroll, which invites the public to enjoy an evening of shopping, dining and local art while supporting local businesses.

3883 Piedmont Avenue
510 653 2473
therarebird.com

SLICER PIZZERIA

Colin Etezadi's Slicer Pizzeria seems innocuous enough—a hip little spot serving slices, whole pizzas, salads and drinks—but this is not the typical pizza joint. An Oaklander of 15 years, with years working at the East Bay's toniest pizza spots under his belt, Colin does things the way we do here in Northern California—he is conscious of where his ingredients come from and is dedicated to using seasonal organic produce and humanely raised meats. The menu changes often, but if given the chance, grab a slice of the Roasted Cauliflower (which includes spinach, red onion, Calabrian chilies and lemon) or Pancetta & Green Garlic (with tomato sauce, shaved fennel, chili flakes and mint) and slide into one of the few seats in the restaurant to enjoy your pizza warm from the oven. "While there are a lot of high-end restaurants around town and in the country, they tend to be more of a time and financial commitment," Colin says. "We wanted to try and get rid of those restrictions and make it more approachable for a larger demographic to have seasonally crafted food."

4395 A Piedmont Avenue
510 808 5424
slicerpizzeria.com

NEIGHBOR

Neighbor seems an apt choice for this store's name on several levels. The store was opened in 2013 by Dana Olson and Karen Anderson, two women who own two shops—Good Stock and Mercy Vintage Now respectively—which are situated right next door to each other on Piedmont Avenue. Neighbor is just steps from the co-owners other two shops, plus, they envision it as a place for home and community. With a warm, inviting feel and a vast backyard under construction—with grand plans, we might add—Neighbor would have to try hard not live up to its name.

Dana and Karen share the buying responsibilities with pleasure, and stock the shop with gifts, artisanal foods, antiques and home décor items that feel timeless, storied and modern

all at the same time. Gas-powered hurricane lamps mingle with modern art coffee table books and hand-woven rugs from Central America. A lifestyle store for the quintessential Oaklander; it's chock full of things you wouldn't find anywhere else with a focus on small brands and vintage, in a warm, friendly shopping environment that instantly makes you feel right at home. Just like a good neighbor.

4200 Piedmont Avenue
510 594 2288
iloveneighbor.com

NATHAN & CO

Nathan Waldon opened his first shop just a block and a half from his current Piedmont Avenue location, in 2006. Two years later, he moved the store into the current space, in a beautiful, historic Julia Morgan-designed building. Nathan tells us, "In the fall of 2011, we opened a second location on College Avenue in Rockridge. When we decided to open a second location, I'll admit, I looked over bridges and through tunnels, but nothing felt like home. So we stayed in Oakland." Nathan describes his shops as "the world's smallest department stores," which isn't too far a stretch, as the shops sell kitchen goods, home décor,

stationery, fragrance, scarves and jewelry, gift books and cookbooks, and gift and toys for the little ones. Nathan explains, "About half of the product crosses over in both stores—I call these the 'basics'—but the rest is unique to that location."

Nathan's passion for the business—and zest for life—is infectious and he tells us, "You don't get into this kind of business to get rich. You do this because you love people, you love design, and you love to serve." A resident of over 12 years, Nathan says, "I'll always live in Oakland."

4025 Piedmont Avenue
510 428 9638
nathanandco.com

GOOD STOCK

Fourth generation Oaklander Dana Olson's easy smile and warm demeanor aren't the only things that draw customers into her shop. Good Stock carries a carefully edited mix of alluring accessories and apothecary products that would thrill even the jaded, "I've seen it all" shopper. "I wanted to focus on the things we adorn ourselves with, things we use, things we pass on, things that remain special to us for as long as we have them," Dana explains. She has quickly built a following for having her finger on the pulse of what's new.

Good Stock has a beautiful vintage glass case filled with covetable, delicate jewelry. The back wall is festooned with beauty products that beg you to slip onto the stool and try fetching new scents and luxe skincare products.

Dana is always scouting for new finds. She currently carries accessory lines Clare Vivier, Calleen Cordero, and Baggu; skin and body care lines include Verso, Rodin, Earth tu Face, and Juniper Ridge.

4198 Piedmont Avenue
510 653 8518
wearegoodstock.com

AFTERWORD

This book reflects the city of Oakland through my eyes. It's not everyone's perception of Oakland, and that's a good thing. Diversity is one of the things that I love most about this city. I created this book because I wanted to show the people of the Bay Area, and the country, that the city is so much more than what they see on the news. I wanted to show them the Oakland that I know.

For the profiles in this book, we often included images of the business owners and their employees, but there are times when they are not visually represented. It is truly the people of this city that make it so enticing, and without their tireless efforts to bring the people of this city an amazing meal, fun night out, or exciting adventure, this book would not have been possible.

Compiling a list of the most interesting places in a city like Oakland, where new businesses are opening every week, can be daunting. I included 90 of my favorite spots in this book, but if we had sent the book to print one month later, Kristen and I could have easily shot and profiled 10 more. Dividing the book up by neighborhoods just seemed to make sense to me, but it also edited out some of the places that I personally adore and frequent regularly. There were also places in the city that are compelling in many ways, but didn't work well for the format of this book or simply weren't available to photograph. For these reasons, I feel obligated to mention a few of those places it pained me to omit.

Bibliomania: I could spend hours at this unassuming shop stacked with thousands of antique books- from vintage cookbooks, first edition novels and classic children's books to quirky, unusual finds like antique yearbooks and vintage cookbooks.

The Oakland Zoo: a zoo that brings families from all over the Bay Area to see the elephants, giraffes and bears and to ride the retro kiddie amusements.

Brown Sugar Kitchen: a homey, Southern-style restaurant that serves up what might be the tastiest, and least forgiving on the waistline, breakfast in Northern California.

The Claremont Resort and Spa: nestled in the Oakland Hills, this grand, historic hotel and spa is one of my favorite places to get a little R&R.

And to the places that opened after we sent the book to print, we're so sorry we missed you.

Melissa Davis

ACKNOWLEDGMENTS

Creating a book takes much more than just an author and photographer. We are so grateful to everyone who helped bring this book to life and out into the world. We extend our deepest gratitude to Liz Siverts for her impeccable taste and designing a book with which we're truly in love, Amy Westervelt and Greg McElhatton for their excellent copy editing skills, Genevieve Isola for fact checking all the tiny details, and Kate Miller and Genevieve Isola for spreading the word about the book across the country.

Thank you to Sharon Montrose, who convinced us that self-publishing was the way to go.

Thank you to the Oaklanders who welcomed us into their businesses and shared their stories with us. You inspire us.

We would also like to thank everyone who contributed to our Kickstarter campaign. You would truly not be holding this book in your hand if it weren't for these very generous individuals. An extra thank you to:

Tina and John McElhatton
Suzanne McElhatton
Eugenia A. Loken
Scott Loken
Scott R. Davis
Robert and Michelle Lane
Rachel and Justin Azama
Valerie Crane Dorfman
Dave and Jodi Murphy
Christopher Davis
Toxtli Design Studios
Linda at East Bay Envy
Margo and John Kieser
Patti Holm, East Bay Sotheby's International Realty
James and Katherine Goodrich
Sandra Jones
Vivian Wang
Rif and Anna
Leslie Santarina at Spotted SF

Rick, Lisa and Elena Hoffman
Cindy Qiu
Lisa Kuhn Seery
Joe Polissky
Alison McLennan
Akaila Johnson
Sandra Jones
Ralph Wolff
Christian Franci
Margaret Willson
Dorian Nasby
Grant Gibson
Will Kivinski
Adrienne Arieff
Elissa Vitale and Doug Edgecomb
Ernesto Crespo-Szabo
Linda Geiser
Jeanine Barnett
Amy Dean
Ruth Stroup

Lauretta and Jeff Skigen

Phyllis Lorenz

BR

Bob Lee

Eleanor Hsu

Erica Hill

Missy Igel

Jenny Collins

Chris Linden

Jeanne Chan

Jill Cannon

Brian Toomajian

Irene Chen

The Weekend Press

Alice Baldridge

Rachel Lyons

Maria Coggiola

Jim G.

Maria MacHatton Pryputniewicz

Dan, Carolyn, Asa and Elana Jay

Uncle Beefy

Jason Brunswick

Jennie Nunn

Jeri Lawson

Jessica L'Esperance

Sasha Bainer

Dolores McElhatton

Olivia Wu

Jessica Sypniewski

Mike Healey

Deidre Joyner

Treena Lombardo

Diana Gil-Osorio

Brian Ahern and Rebecca Peterson

Katie Penn

Daniel Ciruli

Mia Hartvikson

Danielle Demerle

Lesa Wright McHale

Conrad Chuang

Holly Hagen

Michelle Lane

Theresa Spinelli Haines

McElhatton Foley P.C.

Jennifer Marnach

Jason Steinard and Marc Knittel

Jane Haines Ingold

The Amaro Family

Mary Ellen Carroll

Haig G. Mardikian

Daniel Frattin

Ingrid Chen

Joshua Hasten

Nido Kitchen & Bar

Penny and Noel Nellis

Willy Wang and Stacy Tang

NOTES